WHERE IS JOY?

Searching for Peace in the Valley of Grief

by

Joy Martell Souder

For mothers and fathers
who have lost a child,

For the brokenhearted,

For the wounded and desperate.

May you feel God's welcoming arms
as you walk through your own
valley of grief.

TABLE OF CONTENTS

Josh gave Jennifer this picture on her 21st birthday, 2001.

INTRODUCTION

*"Grief is not a process to graduate from,
it is a cyclical journey."*
—Kate Motaung, *Letters to Grief* [1]

I always hated my first name, mainly because no one ever used it. When I heard it used, it didn't sound like me. My middle name is my identifier – **Martell**, a name created by my parents. Any time some little boy learned my first name, he spread the news on the playground, and I would cringe. By the time I got to college, no one used "Joy" when referring to me. In every course, the roll was called on the first day, but no one answered to "Joy Johnson." When I finally realized **my** name being called, I raised my hand to say, "It's Martell." Of course, then I had to spell "Martell" because no one had ever heard that name.

The irony is that I have a lovely first name – **Joy**. I don't think I truly appreciated this name until I read Ann Voskamp's book *One Thousand Gifts*. Now I *want* to use it – I put it on my website and use it in my signature because I truly do feel the **joy** that comes from God's blessings. But it has taken me a long time to find that joy.

The fabric of my life ripped apart in 2002; its purpose, design, meaning, and pattern lay like scraps of fabric. For ten years I asked God, "Where is joy?"

My heart was broken, so I blamed God; He patiently held me, waited for me, loved me. He was the loving Father to an angry and devastated child. This heart is mending – a journey that continues today.

The last time we saw our only child, Jennifer, was the weekend before April 13, 2002. She and Josh were so full of love and excitement, full of plans for the future. It was a delight to be with them.

And in the blink of an eye, the slip of a foot, a crash to the ground, **everything** changed.

The shock and trauma Larry and I experienced, truly understood only by those who have gone through the same tragedy, placed us in the community of parents who have lost a child. Our experience is unique to us just as Jennifer was unique, yet we share many of the same heartaches as other parents in this community.

Broken Hearts

"How Can You Mend a Broken Heart?" by the Bee Gees.

"For My Broken Heart" by Reba McEntire.

"Love Hurts" by Nazareth.

Songs about broken hearts fill the popular song charts of every decade of recorded music. Even country songs about cheating and drinking trace their roots to a broken heart.

But a broken heart can actually be the cause of death after a sudden emotional stress. The Wikipedia entry for "Broken Hearts"[2] refers to research from several respected sources on the medical complications of broken heart syndrome:

- Symptoms that mimic a heart attack such as chest pain or shortness of breath[3]
- Experiencing heartache can result in muscle tightness, increased heart rate, abnormal stomach activity and shortness of breath.[4]
- Grief can precipitate episodes of depression[5] which in severe cases can develop into emotional trauma[6] and even post-traumatic stress syndrome[7].

Perhaps you are reading this book because of your own broken heart because of one of these events:

- a death of a family member, a close friend
- a divorce
- an unfaithful spouse
- a betrayal by a close friend, relative, coworker
- the loss of a job, home (even a move to another city)
- unmet expectations, such as a husband and children
- a diagnosis of cancer or incurable diseases
- the loss of a limb or other significant body part
- trauma from violence (that threatened your safety, the place where you live, work, worship, or where your children go to school)

The broken hearts you and I share may not be from the same circumstances, but we identify with similar feelings, questions, pain, hopelessness, and the inability to change the situation. I reveal my journey, my trauma, my grief, the mending of my broken heart, praying that you find comfort and hope in these words. May you learn through my experience that grief recovery does not travel in a straight line; the peaks and valleys can continue through months and often years.

Each chapter contains a story of my healing and ends with a section of **This I Know Now**. I've also provided space for **Your Turn** to record your prayers and thanks framed in the passage of Philippians 4:6-7:

> *Don't worry about anything; instead, pray about everything. Tell God what you need, and thank him for all he has done. Then you will experience God's peace, which exceeds anything we can understand. His peace will guard your hearts and minds as you live in Christ Jesus. NLT*

These words from the Apostle Paul may feel too simplistic, especially amid grief or trauma, but remember that he was in prison when he wrote them.

Space has been provided for you to respond to one of these suggestions at the end of each chapter. Some days you likely find it impossible to consider any of these practices, but **This I Know Now**: the slow and habitual documenting of what God is doing for you can heal your broken heart. If you do find this practice useful, you might want to purchase a blank journal and follow the pattern.

Larry and I already knew about dying firsthand. We had buried both sets of parents by the 1990s. We knew how to plan funerals, how to sort through belongings, make decisions.

But this? We never expected to bury a child. Not <u>our</u> child!

Chapter 1

APRIL

*Josh and Jennifer bubble with excitement
in anticipation of their special day.*

April 6, 2002

Squeezing ourselves into less space to make room for others, Larry and I stand near the hostess station at Safari's restaurant, just outside Nashville, TN. Conversations swirl around us, names are called, and my cell phone rings.

"Mom, we are running late. We visited a place in Joelton, but we got lost coming back."

"Where are you right now?" I asked.

"Um, I don't really know, some highway, but we're back on track and should be there soon."

We wait a little longer. Josh and Jennifer have spent this Saturday visiting outdoor wedding venues. Their wedding is planned for May 2003, a year from now. Since Josh is working on a Masters' Degree at Virginia Tech while Jennifer finishes her junior year at Tennessee Tech, they plan their weekends carefully. They both really want an outdoor wedding that reflects their love for hiking, rock climbing, and camping.

They finally arrive; we greet with hugs and smiles and are escorted to a nearby booth. In the crowded noisy restaurant, we lean in to hear this important conversation, their faces lighting up our booth. In between drink orders and menu gazing, conversation bounces from Jennifer to Josh and back as they share impressions about three venues. Jennifer's planning folder contains checklists for the preliminary tasks in planning a wedding plus all the information they gathered today.

"The Garden Inn is just perfect; it's a bed and breakfast in Monterey, TN. Since most of our guests are from out of town, the rooms will be perfect for them. They have quite a few restrictions, but the setting is so beautiful," Jennifer explains.

Josh glances at Jennifer and then describes Cheekwood. "It's a beautiful place but much more formal."

"And expensive," Jennifer adds.

"So, what were you looking at in Joelton?" I ask.

We learn The Rawlings in nearby Joelton is in a more rustic setting but has a variety of indoor and outdoor locations. All three locations have information on catering, decorating, music, photographers, and the list gets longer and longer. Despite a long day with delays Josh and Jennifer bubble with excitement in anticipation of their special day.

Through the sharing of the details, we order and eat our meal. Larry and I listen, asking questions, slowly digesting the reality that our only child's wedding day will be next May after her graduation from college.

Jennifer's college life changed drastically in the fall of her junior year. She quit the track team, giving up her track scholarship to be an intern for high school girls for the church she attends in Cookeville. She still loves running and even began training last summer for a triathlon.

In the fall she and Caroline, the other intern, planned and led a retreat for the teen girls, emphasizing inner beauty. Jennifer used a book on hope and living like a butterfly (*hope for the flowers* by Trina Paulus).

Josh and Jennifer spend the rest of the weekend with us before they head back to school. As Jennifer and I work together in the kitchen, we talk about her classes and life with Josh after his move to Virginia Tech. She shares stories about her work with the teenage girls, and some of the struggles "her" girls have. She sees a need for helping teens and young women choose healthy eating as a part of a healthy life. With her new major in nutrition, she tells me some of the ideas she is exploring.

Her voice fills with enthusiasm when she says, "I heard about a program at Vanderbilt that goes to middle schools and high schools to work with girls on self-image and healthy living. That would be a great opportunity. But I also want to help girls have a relationship with God." We try to think of a book for girls that advocates a healthy physical life, social and emotional as well as spiritual life.

"You should write a book about it," I suggest. The writer in me cannot resist.

"I don't know if I can do that."

"Sure, you could. Just write in the same way you talk to girls about the things you have learned and experienced."

The hours fly by, and Jennifer and Josh head back to Cookeville late Sunday afternoon. Josh will still have a long drive to make back to Virginia Tech.

Wednesday Night, April 10

Just before bedtime Jennifer calls me. We chat about school and her field trip to visit a local nursing home to meet a dietitian.

"Mom, please don't let planning my wedding get in the way of our friendship" she begs.

"We won't! Where is this fear coming from?" I ask.

"My roommate is having lots of disagreements with her mother about her wedding. I just don't want that to happen to us."

I can't imagine this since we seldom have big conflicts; we really are good friends. She tells me her plans for the weekend; she and Josh will meet down at his parents' cabin near the Ocoee River. Before we hang up we both say, "I love you."

Saturday Evening, April 13

The Bradford pear tree just outside the front windows of the living room fills the view with white blooms; so dense we can't see the houses across the street. Recent April rain and sunshine provide the perfect recipe for brilliant emerald green grass in Middle Tennessee. Hyacinths have come and gone, and long-stemmed tulips nod in the breeze.

This evening there are only two of us for dinner, so I pull out leftovers from the refrigerator. I grab the ringing kitchen phone as I keep watch over the pots on the stove. A muffled voice is speaking. "Who is this?" I demand. I can't understand who is on the line.

He keeps choking out words, but I finally hear, "It's Josh." A long pause, "This is the hardest phone call I've ever made."

"Josh! What is wrong?"

Larry steps into the kitchen when he hears the alarm in my voice.

"It's Jennifer." His voice breaks, "She's gone." This voice does not even sound like Josh, but I can tell he is crying.

"What do you mean 'gone'?" I look up at Larry who has not moved from his spot. I frantically try to remember Josh and Jennifer's specific plans for Saturday afternoon. "Where are you, Josh?" I ask, raising my voice.

"I'm at the hospital …Jennifer and I were hiking on Starr Mountain, and she fell. They tried to revive her but …she died." Josh can barely choke out his words.

Surely, I heard him wrong, "She's dead? No, that can't be right." Josh is clearly distraught, unable to explain or answer my questions. "Is anyone with you? I need to talk to someone else."

He says his mother is at the hospital with him, and I demand to speak to her. Josh sounds so upset; I foolishly think that his story is just mixed up. Debbie, Josh's mother comes on the phone and explains that Jennifer, Josh, and Katie, his 13-year-old sister, left their cabin that morning and drove a few miles to nearby Cherokee National Forest. They hiked one of the undeveloped trails and climbed to the top of Starr Mountain. As Jennifer headed back down the rough trail, she lost her footing on a precarious section. She fell nearly sixty feet into the dense brush and trees below. Josh and Katie were following right behind her.

At the hospital, doctors continue to exam her even as we are speaking, but Josh's mom encouraged him to call us right away. They promise to call again with more information.

I hang up the phone and just stare at Larry. My brain cannot grasp this trauma. Then I grab Larry and hold on as deep, gut-wrenching sobs rack my body. All I can scream is "NO, NO!" Our lives are splitting apart from this news. One phone call changes everything. The food on the stove continues to cook, forgotten as our hearts are breaking.

Our Jennifer! "How can this be?" loops through my mind. I just talked to her Wednesday night. We have so many questions about her fall, but only Josh can answer those.

Then we think of more immediate questions. How do we get her body home? Where is it taken for the autopsy? Who coordinates all this? Her body is in a hospital almost two hundred miles south of Nashville. We know there is to be an autopsy in Nashville, but we are overwhelmed. How do we handle all these details? Do we have to go down to Cleveland? We pace the living room.

Larry calls Cliff, a friend from church who works part-time at a funeral home. He knew just what to do. All the details are lifted off our shoulders; ten minutes later the doorbell rings.

A dear couple from church we have known since Jennifer was 10 years old enter. Nila was Jennifer's principal in elementary school, and Jerry is the business manager at church. They grab us both with hugs. As I try to talk to Nila, I suddenly feel my chest tightening. The waves of shock are dragging me down.

"I can't breathe. I can't breathe."

This I Know Now:

A broken heart hurts physically. I did not even remember being unable to breathe until I read it in my journal. At the time I didn't understand what was happening to my body, but it seemed to pass quickly. I had no idea that this state, this new normal was shock. Nor did I understand that this was the beginning of a long process, a long journey of grief.

Now I Am Thankful for:

- Larry's strong arms to hold me after the phone call.
- Jerry and Nila coming so quickly to our door. We needed others.
- Our last visit with Jennifer and Josh was filled with joy.

Your Turn:

- Don't worry about ANYTHING, even

_____

- Pray about EVERYTHING
- Tell God what I need
- Thank Him for all He has done.

Philippians 4:6-7

> *Then you will experience God's peace, which exceeds anything we can understand. His peace will guard your hearts and minds as you live in Christ Jesus. NLT*

Chapter 2

STUMBLING

As the mountains surround Jerusalem,
So the Lord surrounds His people.
Psalm 125:2
NIV

Saturday Night

Unanswered questions, perhaps the hardest part of any trauma. We want specifics: Who? When? Why? Where? Tonight, we wait for phone calls from Josh, our only source of information at the moment.

This is the story we learn from Josh, his sister, Katie, and rescue workers.

The three hikers had reached the summit and were on their way down. Jennifer ran ahead of Josh and Katie. She lost her footing and fell nearly 60 feet into the brush. Two men hiking nearby heard shouts and reached Jennifer's side first. One called 911, and the other began CPR. Josh jumped from boulder to boulder trying to reach Jennifer with Katie right behind.

In an interview with a TV reporter, Josh described that moment, "Adrenaline started pounding. I've never prayed so hard or ran so fast, all at the same time." Both Josh and Katie began clearing brush away to make a trail for rescue workers. Jennifer fell into thick brush and trees, away from the trail, making it difficult for rescue workers to reach her.

Rescue workers struggled in their heavy gear to carry a gurney while climbing up the steep mountain. Josh ran down to the workers to help and then back to Jennifer, frustrated with the slow progress of the team heading up the mountain. When they finally reached Jennifer, a rescue worker said she was breathing and had a heartbeat. They quickly placed her on the gurney, and someone continued chest compressions as they struggled back down the mountain. Josh heard one of the workers say her pulse was thready.

About an hour and forty minutes passed from the time she fell to the time they placed her in an ambulance. Twenty-two people from Polk County Rescue Squad along with firefighters from Arkansas in the forest on training exercises assisted in the rescue.

Josh traveled behind the ambulance in the rescue squad chaplain's car, heading to the nearest hospital. It wasn't long until he noticed the sirens and lights are turned off. When the ambulance began stopping at traffic lights, he said, "That's when I knew she was gone."

An autopsy is required in Nashville to determine the exact cause of death. So, we wait as our doorbell rings, and friends from church arrive, so many come that everything becomes a blur of images. I make phone calls to my brothers and other family members; Larry calls his brother in Kansas. We tell the story again and again to each new arrival, in each phone call. Our hearts break each time we begin anew, "Jennifer and Josh were hiking, and she slipped and fell."

The house is full of people who want to help, people who knew Jennifer as she grew up at the Madison church. Some of the women begin cleaning our bedrooms and bathrooms, changing sheets, vacuuming. They are thinking of family and friends who will soon arrive and need places to stay. These details are the last thing on my mind.

Josh calls back to let us know her body is ready to be released. We ask Josh and his mother about their plans to come to Nashville. It seems best for Josh to stay with his parents Saturday night, and they can all travel together Sunday to our house. Josh will drive Jennifer's car home; we haven't even thought about her car. She and Josh both had their cars that weekend since they traveled separately from their universities down to his parents' home.

Cliff made the arrangements through the funeral home to send a van down to the hospital in Cleveland, Tennessee to pick up Jennifer's body. We learn that after the autopsy, we can see her body.

The stream of people entering our house late in the evening changes. Longtime friends from the church we formerly attended across town arrive. One of the church elders gathers everyone around us in the living room, and they sing:

> *"As the mountains surround Jerusalem,*
> *So the Lord surrounds His people."*

Tears flow down my face, but the words comfort me as does his prayer. Time has no meaning, and we don't even remember that we never ate supper. Sometime late that night, my dear friend, Belinda, takes the initiative. She says, "Larry and Martell need to rest, and it would be easier if everyone goes home. George and I will stay with them." I love her for this and appreciate the offer, but Larry and I need to be alone, to digest this trauma.

Two of my brothers, Paul and David, plan to come on Sunday with their wives. I cannot reach Steve, the brother two years younger than me. He lives in West Tennessee; I keep calling his home phone and leaving messages. When I call his cell, there is no answer.

Larry and I are exhausted but after everyone leaves, we need time to just tell each other who we have called, who we want to handle the funeral, all kinds of details we have yet to consider. Once we finally go to bed, both of us wake up several times in the night.

Each time I awaken I think, "It's still true. Jennifer is dead. This is not a dream." Larry says the same thing happened to him.

Sunday Morning

Neither of us feels rested Sunday morning, and we know we have miles to travel as we begin a journey into unknown places. Early that morning I begin calling people in Henderson, Tennessee, who might know Steve's whereabouts. I finally call his church and reach their church secretary. She says Steve and Marie are on a retreat with some college students. The retreat is at a camp in North Alabama with poor cell service. I tell her why I need to reach him, and

13

eventually, she is able to get word to Steve to call me. The signal is not strong when he reaches me; he thinks I said Jennifer has been injured. I finally just shout into the phone, "Jennifer is dead!" His wife, Marie, told me later Steve nearly passed out when he understood me.

When I hang up I sit in the quiet of the kitchen trying to process this new reality. Then I walk out to the driveway to pick up the morning paper and see a neighbor. I tell her what has happened, so she will know why so many cars claim all the parking spots on the street later today.

My Aunt Mayme from Kentucky calls; she tells me she is physically unable to come to Nashville. She is my mother's older sister and among the last of her generation of relatives. Her words remain with me today.

"Martell, just listen to me. I want you to think of Jennifer entering Heaven. Your mama and daddy are there welcoming her home." Tears flow, and I can hardly speak, but I picture them greeting her as they all meet. Sorrow and joy fill my heart at the same moment.

Making Arrangements

This Sunday morning is like no other in our experience; Larry and I don't even plan to go to Sunday School or worship. So many things to do today, to say goodbye to Jennifer.

Our parents died in the 1980's and 90's, so we have planned several funerals. But this one? We never envisioned planning the funeral of our daughter.

So many decisions to make:

- when to schedule visitation and the funeral
- where to have the funeral
- where would we bury her?
- choosing a casket
- when could we see her after embalming?
- when do they need a clean set of clothes for the viewing?

My main thought through all the planning? "Just get it done." I push aside the intense aching in my soul to focus on the pertinent decisions. Dan, a good friend and former minister, comes by to accompany us to the funeral home.

Since Jennifer's body is still in autopsy when we arrive at the funeral home, we take care of other details: choosing a casket, settling on visitation hours to begin at 4:00 P.M. Monday afternoon through Monday night in the small chapel in our church. We want an evening funeral, so Jennifer and Josh's college friends and the high school students she had mentored at their church in Cookeville can come, as well as out of town family and friends and those who work during the day. We plan the funeral for Tuesday night in our church's large auditorium, and the burial on the following morning with family and closest friends. Jerry Sherrill told Larry last night (can it be just yesterday?) that we can have three plots the church owns at a cemetery in nearby Hendersonville.

We are actually eager to have the funeral and be finished with this public part of mourning. Our thoughts can hardly move beyond the Wednesday burial.

Plans are made for an obituary in the newspaper and a program for the funeral; I take on these writing tasks. I find some unique thank-you cards with an insert of a thick handmade paper heart embedded with wildflower seeds. It suggests planting the seeds so when they come up next spring the flowers will be a reminder of Jennifer. These immediately appeal to me; finding ways to express thanks give me a tangible way to cope at this moment.

By the time we return home, the house is full of people who loved Jennifer and love us. Casseroles, vegetable trays, and desserts pour in, and hands are ready to take care of all our needs. Friends take over kitchen duty to organize all the food and keep track of the gifts of love.

During Sunday School this morning one of the adult classes collected a large offering to pay for Jennifer's funeral. Tom, the teacher of the class, comes by with the gift. We are overwhelmed with their generosity, especially since we had not even suggested such a need. Paying for the funeral has not even crossed my mind. During this hectic day Larry and I barely have time to acknowledge one gift before something else interrupts us. I keep reminding myself to write thank-you notes. The moments of the day bring unexpected gifts, phone calls, and friends dropping by showing their love and support.

My youngest brother, Paul, arrives from North Carolina; he drove straight through from his home at the air force base. His family will arrive on Monday. Steve and David, my two other brothers and their wives arrive not long after Paul. Their familiar faces and hugs surround me like a warm quilt, but I keep looking for Josh amid all the faces. My mind returns again and again to Katie, Josh's sister; she witnessed Jennifer's violent death. She is the same age as my middle school students; how is she coping?

Josh finally pulls up in front of our house in Jennifer's little red Hyundai. My heart quickens, and the shaky ground of reality hits me; she is *never* coming home. We have her car parked in the front yard to make space for parking on the street; our neighborhood fills up with vehicles.

I walk out to the street to greet Josh; my main concern is surrounding him with love and compassion, so he knows we place no blame on him for this accident.

His pain is as intense as ours. We cry together in the front yard under the white-blossoms of the pear tree. Then he sees his friends from Cookeville standing nearby. These strong young men embrace Josh — heads bowed, arms wrapped around broad shoulders, weeping. The scene burns into my memory. How they love each other and how they love Jennifer!

I call Jennifer's roommate, Courtney, who is still in Cookeville. We need some clothes for the funeral home as soon as possible. Since Jennifer has lived away from home for three years, I have no idea what is in her wardrobe. I tell Courtney to gather as many clothes as she can and bring them with her. We'll make some selections when I can see the clothes.

Since Jennifer's body is still at the coroner's office, we don't know when we can see her. I have not adjusted to the reality that we will only be looking at her body, not the essence of Jennifer. Unanswered questions hover in the back of my mind, but there is no word all afternoon about the autopsy.

As the afternoon creeps toward evening, I realize I need something appropriate to wear to our daughter's funeral. Brenda and Marie, two of my sisters-in-law, take me to my favorite nearby clothing store. As I try on clothes in the dressing room, I hear a young voice in the stall next to me say, "Mom?" The voice sounds just like Jennifer! My heart leaps. Then another deep ache hits my heart; I swallow that ache and push on. This is not the place to sit down and weep.

After the shopping trip, I come back exhausted – how could that be so tiring? I just push myself to the next task and then the next. There has been no time to reflect on this new coping, physically or emotionally. When I come into the house, my friend, Lark, has a cup of tea ready. I sit while she waits on me – I vaguely realize she is waiting on me in my own house! But I am learning to let others do for me. Somehow, I realize that I am numb from shock and that painful heartrending mourning is yet to come. Just being there makes a difference– "washing my feet."

The Tennessean, our daily paper, calls asking for photos of Jennifer. I find the picture of Josh and Jennifer hiking in the Smokies and set it near the door. Local TV stations call to set up interviews with family. The crowd in our home spills out into the yard, faces changing as some of my family heads back to West Tennessee until tomorrow.

Behind the Scenes

All Sunday afternoon the crowd of people in our living room, dining room, and kitchen shifts and changes. Counters are filled and then pushed into the refrigerator. Two friends take charge of the food, storing it and serving it when needed. Someone brings a cooler of ice and drinks; another brings paper plates and cups. How thoughtful! Friends make sure a list is kept of who brings food. Sometimes I am available to personally thank people for their thoughtfulness, but not always. Sometimes food just shows up with a note, like a coconut cake from a neighbor.

Shana, one of Jennifer's high school youth ministers, pulls me aside and asks me for pictures of Jennifer. She plans to make a slideshow to play during visitation and the funeral. I grab a large box of pictures from upstairs that needs organizing and hand them to her. I just cannot think about pictures now. I hope she can find enough that are useful.

Sunday Night, April 14

Larry and I find a quiet space upstairs to plan the funeral. Earlier in the day we asked Dan to speak and coordinate the service with Keith, our music minister. Larry, Dan, Keith, Josh, and I sit on Jennifer's bed and talk about specific songs she liked, who wants to speak, and music to use in the slideshow.

Larry and I specifically ask this to be a celebration of her life. Josh and Larry both want to speak, but I do not. I know I cannot hold my composure in such an emotional moment. I have plenty of experience speaking in front of large groups of people but sobbing in public is not appealing to me. I will find other ways to share Jennifer's life.

Later that night Larry calls me into his office. The medical examiner is on the phone with results of the autopsy. We listen together on the phone's speaker. The autopsy shows that her spinal cord was severed; he says there is no way she could have regained consciousness.

Slowly the house empties. Larry and I both are exhausted – the emotional swings of the day overwhelm. As the house quiets with only my brother, Paul, sleeping upstairs, details swarm through my mind. Have we told this person? Is this task taken care of? I finally close my eyes to sleep, knowing tomorrow will be just as full of decisions and shifting emotions as today.

This I Know Now:

The day was a blur of people and activities, but many scenes of love remain in my memory. I can't imagine making it through this experience without the support of family and friends. I don't remember disagreements or arguments or angry feelings; we were united in supporting each other during this nightmare of reality

Now I Am Thankful for:

- Friends who took care of details, making sure we ate.
- College friends who surrounded and supported Josh.
- God holding me through this day of shock.

Your Turn:

- Don't worry about ANYTHING
- Pray about EVERYTHING, especially

_____

- Tell God what I need
- Thank Him for all He has done.

Philippians 4:6-7

> *Then you will experience God's peace, which exceeds any-thing we can understand. His peace will guard your hearts and minds as you live in Christ Jesus. NLT*

Chapter 3
REUNION

We just trust that he'll be glorified,
even in the things we can't understand.

Monday, April 15, 2002

Another beautiful spring day! I walk outside to pick up the morning paper. I open it and show Larry Jennifer's picture and a story on the front page. The story provides the details of her death, some we did not know. Despite the uninvited attention we are just glad our friends in Nashville will get the news of her death in case they have not heard.

This morning becomes a whirlwind to get things done as the house fills with family and friends. We delegate many of the details of the day to the willing hands that surround us: locating places for family members to stay, picking up family at the airport, managing the food that continues to pour in, answering the phone, delivering Jennifer's clothes to the funeral home.

And then, a phone call from the funeral home. Her body is ready for us. Who will go? Does Josh want to go? Do we want someone to go with us?

Josh decides to stay at our house to prepare for a television news team coming to interview him. Larry and I decide to go alone to see her body. Courtney, Jennifer's roommate, helped me choose a soft pink turtleneck sweater to dress

Jennifer; the funeral director tells us it is a perfect choice because she has a lot of bruising around her neck. I gaze at our beautiful young daughter but feel nothing. This lifeless form is not Jennifer. Without her megawatt smile, the body before us is just a shell. Her spirit, her soul is gone. And I do not cry. Our beliefs give us confidence that she is with her Father in Heaven, and this body will decay.

Monday Afternoon

Press Time

Time is swiftly getting away from us.

Two television news crews arrive and set up in the backyard. Josh agreed to an interview; his good friends, Robert and Courtney, Robert's girlfriend and Jennifer's roommate, sit with him in support. I watch from the deck as Josh struggles to find the right words to describe his loss; he is so strong, but he breaks my heart. He retells the events of Saturday afternoon when they hiked to the top of Starr Mountain. When Jennifer looked out over the rolling peaks of the Smokies she told Josh, "This is the most beautiful place you've ever taken me." Minutes later he heard her scream and ran down the trail to reach her; he said he had never prayed so hard or ran so fast.

Josh shared some of the highlights of Jennifer's mission work while being interviewed, as well as her work as a youth intern with the church in Cookeville. "I never deserved to be with her, and I realize that. I was fortunate to have the time I had with her. I feel lucky for that."

When Josh drove Jennifer's car back to our house, he found her Bible in the front seat. It was marked with a verse in Daniel. He says, "We just trust that He'll be glorified, even in the things we can't understand."

But the saddest words Josh spoke, "What do you do when the person who you tell everything to is gone?"

The local TV stations carried stories of Jennifer's death as well as the interview with Josh on their evening newscast. We set the VCR to record them to be sure we will see them.

Before we know it, we are scrambling to get ready for Visitation at 4:00. I gather some significant items that represent Jennifer's life before we pile into cars and drive to the church building. Details fall into place; tasks are taken over by willing hands. Church staff set up tables in the lobby where we can place Jennifer's memorabilia. Liz, Jennifer's sixth-grade teacher who is also my dear friend, takes Jennifer's hiking boots, pictures, -- all the memorabilia and arranges it with her artistic eye. Copies of memory sheets are placed on tables with pens. The slideshow chronicling her life with the music Josh selected is ready to play in the chapel.

A Private Moment

Our extended family and Josh's family assemble in Bixler Chapel before the doors are opened so we can view the casket privately. This tragedy overwhelms us all, but we are confident that Jennifer has gone to her home in heaven. The faith of both families gives us a foundation to lean on.

Before Jennifer and Josh began their hike Saturday, she handed him her engagement ring for safe-keeping. As we stand around her casket he returns it to her finger. My mind takes a picture of each of these moments to look at later. A line is gathering, and we need to begin.

Reunions

The next few hours feel like a marathon race. The line of people soon stretches out the door of the small chapel in our church and winds through the lobby.

Larry and I stand with Josh at the front of the chapel to meet friends who come to share our grief: church friends from the places we worshipped in Nashville, my work friends from various Nashville schools, Larry's work friends, teenagers and college students from Nashville, Jennifer and Josh's college and summer camp friends, more family members from out of town. Hours pass as people hug our necks, love us, and weep with us. Each memory shared pulls me back out of the waters of despair.

Sometimes we laugh together at silly stories; sometimes we just hold on to each other. Other times I walk to the casket to stand with close friends, but Larry soon reminds me of the other people who are waiting.

By 7:00 P.M. my neck and shoulder muscles are locking up from constantly reaching up to people, so I ask for a stool. Supper is provided by the Ladies Bible Class, but I can barely eat. Youngest brother, Paul, gives me a shoulder rub. When the music and slideshow stop, Josh turns to me and says, "I need to see those pictures. It keeps me close to her."

And people keep coming. We hear story after story from mothers and fathers, telling us how Jennifer made an impact on their son or daughter's life. One mother says, "She called me from camp one night to tell me my daughter wanted to be baptized." Jennifer was a camp counselor during her high school years for our church camp, but I never heard this story.

Family members stay with us throughout the evening and guide us home to get some sleep. For hours we laughed, wept, hugged, and loved on the people who came, but now I am empty. I move in a fog, no more energy to cry or think or remember.

When our family doctor came through the line, he asked if I needed something for sleep. I thought about my restless sleep last night and decide I need some rest. He later handed me a prescription, and someone made sure it was filled. When I get home, I take it and wait for sleep to end this day.

Tuesday, April 16

A new day finds me mentally going through the list of "to-dos": finish the program for the funeral, be sure Larry has time to prepare his comments for the funeral, be at the church building before 4:00 for the final viewing, and then, the funeral.

The reality of this day does not sink in. Perhaps shock protects me from consciously accepting this truth – Jennifer is dead, and today is her funeral.

The house fills again with family and friends, ready to do anything to make this day a little easier. Food continues to arrive; someone is always in our small kitchen to store food, arrange some to be eaten at any time and keep a written record of these gifts from open hearts. Neighbors we only know by a nod or a raised hand leave food on the porch.

I hear a lawn mower and look out the window to see Gary, Larry's brother, mowing the grass. I am sure no one asked him to do it, but he saw a need and took care of it.

Larry spends some time in the quiet of his office to write his comments for the funeral. I'm at the computer in my upstairs office organizing the order of the program so it can be copied. I place a picture of Jennifer and Josh with a rainbow behind them on the front page. I tried to express in a few words how much she experienced in her young life.

> *Her days were brief but brimmed over with joy and love and service to God and others.*
>
> *Jennifer approached life with a spirit of adventure and perseverance. She traveled to numerous places with church groups on mission trips and always found adventure. She taught Bible school to Jamaican children, built an addition to a house in Morant Bay, built church buildings in Mexico, taught Bible in Venezuela, led teenage girls' retreats and served as camp counselor in Christian youth camps. Along the way she climbed the Rockies, jumped cliffs in Jamaica, hiked in Venezuela, backpacked in the Smokies, ran track meets for Tennessee Tech, mountain-biked trails throughout Tennessee and trained for a triathlon in Knoxville to be held later this summer.*

Marathon #2

When we arrive at the church building Tuesday afternoon for the second visitation, a large crowd is already assembled. It seems as large as the crowd on Monday. This time we see friends from our past, along with extended family and friends from Texas, Kentucky, Indiana, Colorado, and Ohio. However, many faces are unexpected: BJ's parents (one of my students from a former class of students with special needs), teachers from other schools where I once taught, a roommate from my college days, Jennifer's kindergarten teacher, the president at Tennessee Tech, the preacher who baptized Jennifer, our neighbors.

The sea of faces and hugs begin to blur, but I want to remember each face and hug. I just hope everyone signs the registration book. When I slip out of the chapel for a minute, I see people writing memories on the blank sheets we provided.

Teens from Cookeville

I notice a large crowd arriving in the lobby; the teenagers from her church in Cookeville have arrived with a long colorful banner filled with personal memories written by each teenager. They hang it on the windows in the corridor just outside the chapel for all to see. The high school girls wear brightly colored paper butterflies pinned to their dresses, reminders of a lesson Jennifer taught them. It was at a retreat earlier in the year: Beauty Within, focusing on life with Christ at the center symbolized by the butterfly.

Notes from the Banner

- Addison: Every time I saw your daughter she was smiling and every time I saw her, she just made my day.
- Jill: Jennifer lived every day as though it were her last. Yet she also had such an ambition for her future. She was going to write a book with Caroline about living healthy inside and out. She wanted it to help girls who were middle-school and high school age to help them have self-esteem and to help them know what life really is! She always encouraged me to follow my dream and be myself. She was never fake.
- Olivia: Jennifer has been a blessing since the day that I met her. I have never met a more encouraging person. She taught me to be a "butterfly." Thank you for allowing her to come here and bless us.
- Charles: Although she was an "intern" and I held the title "minister" she taught me so much more than I ever taught her. Your daughter made a difference with our teens, college students, and church family. She continues to be a light to me.
- Kittrell: She taught me more things about God and life than any teacher ever could.

We do not know these teens, but they knew our Jennifer. Their parents have come through the line with their own stories of Jennifer's influence. One mother said that Jennifer's example in good food choices led her daughter to pick carrots over chocolate. When the teens met for supper at fast food restaurants,

Jennifer took her own healthy food. These high school teenagers and college friends loved her and want us to know how much she impacted their lives.

I just keep pushing through the minutes and hours; tissues always close by. After three hours of visitation, we suddenly realize it is time for the funeral. I take some deep breaths as the funeral home workers clear the chapel.

This I Know Now:

The interaction with nearly 1000 people over two days was exhausting, and I cried so much I sounded like I had a cold. But the stories gave us a new perspective on Jennifer and how God used her life. Despite the stress, my faith and family held me together.

I put the Scripture below on the funeral program, but today I have a more complete understanding of how the Lord renewed my strength.

> *"But those who hope in the Lord will renew their strength. They will soar on wings like eagles; they will run and not grow weary, they will walk and not be faint." Isaiah 40:31 NLT*

Now I Am Thankful for:

- The memories of Jennifer shared on the banner. I put them in a memory book and still have them.
- Hands that took care of many details those days and I never knew it.
- A foundation of faith in God that supported me.

Your Turn:

- Don't worry about ANYTHING
- Pray about EVERYTHING
- Tell God what I NEED, not what I want

_____

- THANK Him for all He has done.

Philippians 4:6-7

> *Then you will experience God's peace, which exceeds anything we can understand. His peace will guard your hearts and minds as you live in Christ Jesus. NLT*

Chapter 4
CELEBRATION

*This quiet little girl touched so many people
with her gentleness, her patience, her service.*
—Kevin Teasley

Tuesday Night, April 16

Larry, Josh, and I wait until each member of our extended families gathers around Jennifer's casket one more time. We stand with Josh as he takes the engagement ring from her finger and says goodbye. By now my energy reserves are on empty and looking at her body does not feel like goodbye. I look at the shell of a beautiful spirit we loved so dearly, but I am numb. We step away from the casket and join the family.

It helps to see the faces of Cliff and Tom, church members who also work for the funeral home, taking care of closing the casket and preparing it to be moved.

Our extended family leaves the chapel first and find their places in the front of our main auditorium. I can hear singing from the auditorium. The casket is rolled out of Bixler Chapel, through the lobbies, followed by the pallbearers, some of Josh's closest friends from Tennessee Tech.

Larry, Josh, and I follow the casket. When we enter the auditorium, I see the seats on the first floor are filled; I look up to see more people in the balcony.

We ran out of the programs, so we know there were over 1000 people in attendance. Jennifer's peers from the Madison church (college students and the Youth group) and college students and teens from the Collegeside Church in Cookeville are honorary pallbearers, so they are sitting together.

While the audience waited for us, the slideshow of pictures played on the big screen. Josh selected the background music, a recording of "You Are Holy" sung by campers at Kamp Kanakuk, where he and Jennifer worked in the summer.

I'm trying to take in everything I see and hear, noticing familiar faces as we walk in. Larry, Josh, and I sit on the first row with Josh's parents and sisters nearby.

Opening Prayer at Jennifer's funeral

Dan Dozier, family friend and minister begins the service with a prayer. His first words touch my heart,

> *"We need you here with us in this time of loss. We need your strength. We long for your comfort. We yearn for your peace." After the prayer he addresses the family in behalf of the whole audience, "What we are attempting to do, as best we know how, is stand beside you in your grief. Even if our words make it clear that we really do not understand, we hope you will hear our hearts more than our words. We want to be near you in your loss…So as a way of honoring her memory and as a way of celebrating her beautiful life we are going to do that which Jennifer loved to do – we are going to worship. We are going to sing songs that Jennifer loved – songs that express the faith and trust in the Lord on Whom she built her life."*

Keith Lancaster and a praise team lead the whole church in singing the hymns we selected. I feel supported by an overwhelming feeling of love from this body of people who are connected to our family. When the whole body lifts their voices in praise to God, I block out my sorrow and find myself singing many of the songs with joy.

Tribute from Friends

Shana, one of Jennifer's youth ministers during high school shared the metamorphosis Jennifer went through from middle school to high school and then college. She remembered the quiet, shy freshman she met years ago. "I first saw the light come into Jennifer's eyes sitting in a little sweltering church in Jamaica one summer. Lauren and Jennifer were leading seventy-nine four-year-olds singing: 'I just want to be a sheep, baa, baa' in Vacation Bible School. She just blew me away; I saw something in Jennifer I'd never seen before.

When I saw her a few months ago, she told me about Josh, "He is the godliest man I know, and he wants nothing more for me than to go to heaven with him and be pure in our relationship." That's what she loved about Josh.

She came a long way from the quiet little girl in Bible class to leading a girls' retreat at Tech.

Conn Hamlett, Jennifer's high school Bible and history teacher also watched her positive transformation to more outgoing and outreaching while maintaining her core of kindness and goodness. "What a beautiful butterfly of a person."

Tory Treadway, Youth Minister and camp director at Madison knew Jennifer as a camp counselor but also as a babysitter for two of his special needs children. He and Kim trusted Jennifer to handle their needs. Brittany, especially, loved to talk to Jennifer.

Sonya Mansfield, Jennifer's high school track coach speaks of Jennifer's determination and perseverance in track practice. She tells a story of Jennifer staying late at practice, running with a parachute behind her, getting in as much training as possible.

Courtney Earles, Jennifer's college roommate, Kelly Campbell, minister in Cookeville, and her fiancé, Josh, share their thoughts.

Kevin Teasley, a minister from Cookeville who planned to counsel Josh and Jennifer before their wedding captured my heart with his insights of where Jennifer is now.

> *If Jennifer were here she would say the way to honor her*
> *was to honor her God.*

*Jennifer's high school
senior picture, 1998.*

*Jennifer and Courtney,
Spring Break beach trip*

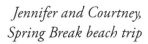

Wednesday night Jennifer and I talked about her wedding, talked about the pre-marital counseling I would do with her and Josh. A year from now she would be a bride right here in this church, a beautiful, radiant, dazzling bride. But the glory of a wedding would just be a rehearsal for the wedding of the Bridegroom Christ when He comes again.

She had a smile that could fill up a room. Right now, she sits under the smile of a loving Father, and she is discovering how wide and how high and how deep is the love of Jesus for her. God would welcome her by saying, "Let's celebrate because my child has come home."

Larry speaks last to thank all those who came to the service, all those who have offered us help. He shares an observation about himself. "I've become a hugger in the last few days. You know that is not typical of me, but we need each of you to help us through this time." He ends with this thought, "She's graduated to glory."

My heart is brimming over with joy, delight, and hope, but tears spill over with some of these stories.

The last song, "When the Night is Falling," we sing ends with this chorus:

When this life is over, and the race is run,
I will hear you calling,
Come, I will come while you sing over me.

Long lines of teenagers and college students, the honorary pallbearers, exit the auditorium first, lining the lobby as her casket slowly rolls up the aisle. Our friend, Turner, plays "Amazing Grace" on his bagpipes.

Before the funeral, I thought I would greet more people in the lobby, but as we follow her casket out of the auditorium, my plan soon feels like a mistake. As hundreds of people spill into the lobbies I am overwhelmed by the bodies and noise.

All my senses are on overload; I don't see Larry anywhere. I must get out of this crowd! I know if I don't get away, I will fall to pieces. Desperately searching faces, I see one of my brothers, don't even remember which one. I'm sure he sees the panic on my face and helps me out of the crowd.

Tuesday Night

Following the funeral, Larry and I try to be in two places at once. He finds me somehow in all the confusion of a crowded lobby to let me know he invited his family from Indiana to our house. At the same time, some of the friends of Josh and Jennifer have gathered in the church fellowship hall for a meal prepared for us. I feel the need to visit with Josh's friends, as well as show my appreciation to those who brought food for all of us.

After eating a bit, I head home to see more family. My mind and body are ready to shut down. Tomorrow morning, we bury Jennifer, and I can't think. I'm not sure who is heading home tonight and who is staying over for the burial tomorrow. It is a struggle just to drive home and talk to more family, no matter how much I love and appreciate them coming.

Larry and I eventually fall into bed, totally exhausted. Gary and Ruthann are still staying with us.

Wednesday Morning, April 17

Saying Goodbye

One of our friends offers his limo to drive us to the cemetery this morning. Josh's family meets us at our house, and we ride together in the limo to the Hendersonville cemetery. A small group of family and friends gather at a grave provided by our church. Sometime in the last few days, Larry came out to the cemetery to see where the plot is located. I like the feeling of this place as we stand beneath a large tree while Dan makes a few remarks. This is all I need, a quiet and low-key time, after the long, crowded day on Tuesday. Josh's family leaves after the burial as did most of our out-of-town friends and family.

We invite everyone to come back to the house; we know we'll find plenty of food, but most everyone leaves town right away. When I walk into our living room, every empty space overflows with flower arrangements and plants. I thought we left enough at the church and graveside that we would not have so many. This is overwhelming, so much cluttering my mind and our home.

My heart is full of memories of dear friends and family, their compassion, people we did not even know who were impacted by Jennifer's life. Exhaustion weighs on me physically: a face raw from crying, a headache from stress, and a body functioning on too little sleep.

Once everyone is gone, the silence overwhelms me. I restlessly wander the house and then try to nap; I have little interest in food or doing anything to distract myself. Being a plant person, I consider sorting through the flowers and plants that crowd my living room, but lethargy has sapped all my strength. I do not even think about going back to teaching. I barely think about my students or lessons the substitute needs. I don't care.

I sit on our deck and replay the days since Saturday, April 13; it's only been four days. A movie flashes in my mind of faces, bits of conversations, warm hugs, offers to help. So many moments from those hectic days are blurred, and I need to replay them in my head.

This I Know Now:

Despite needing to be alone after days filled with people, I found myself not knowing what to do with myself. Those four days were about doing "the next thing" and now there were no more "next things." My thoughts returned to the funeral because I felt such comfort in everyone's memories. Wangerin's description of shock after trauma certainly described me. "Shock must stun the mind to silence a while…to disengage the intellect."[8]

Now I Am Thankful for:

- The comfort of knowing God was glorified through Jennifer's death.
- Thousands of people know that her life was a holy sacrifice to God our Father.

- Family members who drove and flew great distances to be with us.

Your Turn:

- Don't worry about ANYTHING
- Pray about EVERYTHING
- Tell God what I NEED
- THANK Him for all He has done.
- In my circumstance today, I may not be able to see His gifts and blessings, but I can find at least three blessings today.

_____

_____

_____

Philippians 4:6-7

> *Then you will experience God's peace, which exceeds anything we can understand. His peace will guard your hearts and minds as you live in Christ Jesus. NLT*

Chapter 5
HEARTBROKEN

Tears are raining down my cheeks,
and I just want a place to let go.
My car is safe,
and I can sob and weep alone.

Wednesday Night

We have a wonderful worship service each Wednesday night in Bixler Chapel; it always feeds my soul. I decide to go tonight, even though Larry does not. I find joy tonight in the worship and sing with the congregation songs of praise to God. Near the end of the service, an older mother comes forward and asks for prayers. She lost a daughter not too many months ago. Her tender heart needs comfort from brothers and sisters.

As I leave after the service, a friend sitting behind me tells me I am so brave! But out in the lobby, I run into Joy, a friend I did not see during visitation. Her boys and Jennifer are near the same age, and we spent many a service together in the nursery when our babies needed some time to toddle about. She grabs me and hugs me so tightly, telling me how sorry she is. Suddenly, I lose my control and rush away. Tears are raining down my cheeks, and I just want a safe place to let go. My car is safe; I sob and weep alone. I know my exhaustion keeps all my feelings on the surface. When I get home, I fall into bed.

Thursday, April 18

Emalie calls me early and asks, "What are you doing today?"

"I don't know." I'm still numb, haven't made any plans, don't have a desire to do anything.

"Why don't you come with me today? I need to stop by my office and then we can do whatever you want," she says.

"I do need to buy some thank you notes."

"Great! I'll come pick you up in an hour," She sounds as positive as ever. Emalie has been my best friend for several years. We taught together at Two Rivers Middle and then we transferred to the new Donelson Middle School two years ago. She now works as support staff for new teachers assigned to her.

After we hang up, I wonder why I said "yes." I have no energy to do anything. Larry is a bit surprised, but since he has missed several days of work, he plans to go to work. He needs to spend some time on the most pressing things.

We drive to Emalie's office with little conversation. As we encounter people I don't know, Emalie tells them who I am. This turns into "Oh, I am so sorry" conversation. I say as little as possible. I am typically an outgoing person, but I. Have. Nothing. No energy or desire to engage in social politeness. None of this bothers Emalie; she is just with me and that is enough. After lunch we find a stationery store and I pick out some thank-you cards. Suddenly, I am wiped out. It's time to get home and be alone.

I am grateful that Emalie took me out because it helped a little. She is an easy person to have as a friend, no demands or expectations.

O God, you are my God!
This burden is so heavy.
Turn my ashes into a crown.

Monday, April 22

Days begin to blend together. I don't know what to do with myself. I love to read, always have a stack of library books, but nothing appeals to me. I am not interested in TV or listening to music. Can't talk to friends, so I find myself on the deck again replaying the movie in my head.

This whirlwind of trauma is disorienting, words just float around me, taking up air. My heart feels like it will explode, the tears will not stop, my head aches, and I wander from room to room looking for her. She will never come in the front door again. My heart aches.

I slowly begin sorting through Jennifer's clothes and other belongings. I want them to be useful to others, so I give away as much as possible to her college friends. Jennifer is our only child, and I keep thinking, "Who am I saving this for?" Some of these items might mean something to her friends. Jennifer and Courtney lived in an apartment in Cookeville so there are more loose ends we need to tie up. Larry and I will need to go to Cookeville to move her furniture and other belongings out of the apartment and bring them back to Nashville.

I begin writing in a journal; I process everything better if I write it down. My practice of journaling depends on whether school is in session. I usually slack off during the busy school year and pick it up again in the summer. Sitting on the deck in the early morning I write my first journal entry on May 20, seven days after her death. Spending time in prayer and Bible study completes this morning routine. The journals allow me to reconstruct this journey through grief.

Journal Entry:

> *Lord, do you feel my heavy heart?*
>
> *My chest is tightening as the elephant gets heavier and heavier. I have mourned from my innermost being these last few days, but now this aching heart must be physically breaking. O, my soul!*

This vaguely familiar heaviness in my chest reminds me of something, but I can't remember it. Then a slim paperback book arrives in the mail from Amazon. Gary, Larry's brother, sent us this book: *When There Are No Words: Finding Ways to Cope with Loss and Grief* by Charlie Walton.[9]

Just glancing at the chapter titles tells me this book has valuable information.

It feels like a treasure box of answers as I read the list.

I search for the author's story and learn two of his teenage sons died at the same time of carbon monoxide poisoning. First, I realize his story is more traumatic than mine and second, he has the benefit and wisdom of time. Each chapter provides practical advice and puts words to so many of my feelings and conflicting emotions. Above all, the book gave me permission to *have* all these feelings.

His chapter, "Two Cement Blocks, Ready to Wear," describes the heavy feeling on my chest so clearly. I remember having this feeling earlier in my life, but I didn't know what to call it.

For months after my mother died in 1994, my chest carried the same heavy feeling. I never identified it as grief or sadness; I just thought I was tired all the time. Mother suffered two years with cancer as she went in and out remission. After the last return of the disease, she chose not to be treated again. Each death is different, and the grieving is different. When my father died ten years before, I grieved but with some joy that he would no longer suffer. Mother was a close friend; I felt orphaned when she died.

Now, when that same heaviness settles in my chest, I know <u>its name</u> – Grief.

Each chapter in Walton's book helps me understand grief a little better. Two chapters proved especially helpful during those first days: "Let People Do Things" and "Every Hug Dilutes the Pain."[10]

This I Know Now:

- Reading my journal entry allows me to peek into my head and heart in those early days of grief. This is what I wrote on April 20:

In my Bible study today of gratitude I realize that IF I can praise God daily for the gift of Jennifer's life, I can keep His purpose in perspective.

Lord, her life was a gift from the very beginning. Her birth was a miracle, and I never thanked you enough. Eventually, I just took this gift for granted and became absorbed in the everyday.

I marvel at how you used her from the first days of her involvement with the teens at Madison. Each year provided a building block to strengthen her faith, her trust, her service, and her example. It all became a beautiful tapestry of a life dedicated to her Father.

- Charlie Walton's book is absolutely the best book for the early days of grief; even though he is no longer alive, his book is available on Amazon. I give it away so much that I can't keep a copy on my shelves.
- "Sitting Shiva" has great benefits for a grieving person. My friend, Rose, told me about it much later, but even then, I'm not sure I completely understood the benefits until I read Miriam Greenspan's book.[11] "Sheva" in Hebrew means seven, and in this ancient Jewish practice mourners stay at home for seven days after the burial of a loved one. Friends bring food and drink and sit with the mourner to give the mourner opportunities to voice their grief. The key to this practice is the "sitting," not the talking by visitors to fill the quiet space. Our culture has difficulty allowing sadness to permeate a mourner's body and soul. Sitting with someone in quiet challenges many who want to say words of comfort.
- After the seven days mourning continues for thirty days but in a less intense way. For the next eleven months, the mourner's prayer is said twice a day.
- How can "sitting Shiva" work today? I would visit the home of a close friend or relative who is mourning with a simple dessert, finger food, or soup (especially in fall or winter). I would

explain that I came to sit, not give advice, but to listen or to just be with him or her. I would take my Bible that has the lament psalms highlighted, but I would take my cues from the mourner. The object is to be as quiet and reserved as possible but available to meet the needs of the grieving person.

Now I Am Thankful for:

All these people who were active in the weaving of Jennifer's life:

- teachers at Goodpasture Christian School
- the life coaches and youth ministers for the Madison Youth Group
- camp counselors and directors and the church at Collegeside in Cookeville
- Thank you, Lord, for good days and for hard days. I know I am healing. I can feel the prayers all around me.

Your Turn:

- Don't worry about ANYTHING, even

  _____

- Pray about EVERYTHING
- Tell God what I need
- Thank Him for all He has done.

Philippians 4:6-7

> *Then you will experience God's peace, which exceeds anything we can understand. His peace will guard your hearts and minds as you live in Christ Jesus. NLT*

Chapter 6
LONGING

*A deep, deep ache of longing fills me
for the child and the woman who is gone.
I just can't believe she is gone forever.*

May 2002

School has not been in the forefront of my mind since April 13, but I want to see my eighth graders before the school year ends. I think some of them might have questions for me, and we need some closure. We've been together their last year in middle school, a journey is nearly completed. These students are mine for only a few short months before they make the giant leap into high school.

After teaching students with special needs for twenty-two years, I returned to "regular" education, teaching eighth grade language arts the last four years. I began using seminars throughout the school year to discuss critical questions and topics from our literature studies and decide to return for a seminar with each class. The Socratic Seminar is a highly structured teaching strategy to engage students in critical thinking. Routines are established early in the year with students seated in a large circle around the classroom. A question is presented, usually about a novel we have read, and each student is expected to respond. I pass around a stone etched with the word, "peace"; only the person holding the stone can speak. Civility, respect for other opinions, and thoughtful responses are valued.

I know my low energy level prevents me from functioning for a whole day of school, so I'll divide my visit into two days.

Thursday, May 9

My first visit begins today after lunch for the last two periods. When Travis, one of my "loud" students, sees me in the hall, he grabs me, nearly knocking me over with a big hug. No doubt he will spread the word that I am back.

During my planning period, my substitute helps me arrange the desks in two circles for the seminar. I set up the TV equipment to show one of the local TV station's stories of Jennifer's death.

The bell rings, and fifth period students enter --- quite noisy and loud. As they settle down, I remind them of the Seminar standards – only one person speaks at a time. A seminar works well when students know the expectations and practice them; we had several seminars throughout the year, so I feel confident this will work today.

First, I play the video tape which summarizes the events surrounding Jennifer's death. I then read aloud the editorial written about her life from the Tennessee Tech student newspaper. Next, I pass out individual funeral programs; all eyes focus on the programs, and silence fills the room. Then I light a candle to signify the official beginning of Seminar.

At first only a few questions are posed:

- How did you feel when you found out?
- How are you handling this?
- Do you want to be alone sometimes?
- Was the funeral sad?
- Did you pick out her clothes?
- How did she slip?
- How did you feel when the dirt was on top of the casket?

Too many of my students know about traumatic deaths from the inner city; family members, friends, and neighbors often are targets of violence. No matter where they live, inner city or suburbs, my students experience a steady diet of family drama. Their questions indicate a curiosity in the details surrounding death; I watch their reactions and notice heads nodding in affirmation as they mentally compare their own experiences with mine.

Their questions fill the entire period; all the students are serious, respectful, and interested. My talkative sixth period surprises me with their constraint today. They ask similar questions as fifth period.

A few different questions asked are:

- Do I think Josh will be a part of our lives?
- How did we treat him when we saw him the first time?
- Did I have a Seminar to get this off my chest or to be done with it?

Seminar allows all questions to be considered if asked seriously and respectfully. I answer each question carefully. At the end of the period I suddenly realize my body is tight from the tension and strain of the last two hours. I've learned to expect the unexpected with middle school students, but I am pleased they handle this serious subject with dignity and respect.

As soon as I get home, I head straight to the couch in the living room. Courtney comes by later to bring us the money she received when she sold Jennifer's textbooks. The money surprises us, and we tell Courtney to keep it. We had not even thought about these little details of completing a life. We talk about her plans for the apartment, paying bills, and finishing up the semester.

She shares details about her wedding plans for December; Larry tells her he will video her wedding as our gift to her and Robert. Courtney's eyes widen, staring at Larry. She stammers, "You don't have to do that."

"It's what I do part-time, and I want to do this," Larry says. I nod and smile in agreement. What a great idea! This is the best way we can show her how much we love and appreciate her. Before she leaves, she wants to show me her wedding dress. Very classic, simple style, she calls it "Jackie O" style --- a perfect for no-fuss-or-frills Courtney.

Friday, May 10

I return to school for Seminar with my first period and second period students. The first period students have very little to say except for Tony. He reads a touching paragraph he has just written and later reads a poem he wrote.

Second period begins immediately with questions and continue until the end of class bell:

- Did I think about suing the park or the ambulance people?
- What were the last words we said to each other?
- Has this brought me closer to God or farther away?
- Did I sometimes walk by her room and stop and remember?
- What did I do that whole week after her death?

I explained that sometimes I just sat and replayed the events in my head.

Andrew, a student who saw his father kill his mother asks, "Do you sometimes think everything is fine and then other times realize that it is not?"

"Exactly," I answer.

Before I leave school, I stop by the main office to see Rob, my principal, and Damon, our assistant. Damon asks if I've thought about when or if I will come back before school is out. I really have not. He advises me to take care of myself — do whatever I need for now. Rob tells me to get a letter from my doctor if I need to take more time. I am almost out of sick days, and our system provides only four bereavement days.

Their advice makes sense to me since I have not made any plans – so unlike me. I always plan ahead, but the days since Jennifer's death feel like I am operating in another dimension.

On the way to my car, I stop by the gym to see some of my students, since they are in P.E. class. I open the gym door to the sound of a barrage of bouncing basketballs. I stand just inside the door. Everything is bouncing – noises, voices, and balls. Suddenly I am disoriented, light-headed and weak-kneed. If I don't get away from this pandemonium, I'll collapse. I get to my car as quickly as I can and sit in the silence.

What is wrong with me? I've never felt like this, noise that overwhelms all my senses. On the way home, I stop by the church building, and happen to see Frank in the parking lot. He directs the church counseling ministry, so kind and interested in the welfare of others. I share this disorienting experience with him. He reminds me, "Martell, you suffered a trauma. This is not unexpected."

His words remain with me as I drive home to safety, security, and quiet. I finally sort out these feelings and come to this new understanding: my mind expects me to function as it did *before* her death. I must learn how to function with this new reality *after* her death. I feel fragile and breakable.

Once I am home I realize going back to school and talking to my classes took more out of me than I thought. I take a nap before I pack up to drive to David's house in West Tennessee for the weekend. Steve and his wife will also be there. Larry asked me if it would be okay if he didn't go. Small talk is Larry's least favorite thing to do, and I often visit family alone. I'm fine with this arrangement for this weekend.

I water all the plants from the funeral and take one more phone call before I leave town. It is Emalie. "Do you need any help?" It's comforting to know she is thinking about me.

Saturday, May 11

At David's, the gentle rhythm of spring in the country soothes my soul. Tall wind chimes sway from the front porch, sounding like church bells. We sit outside, prepare lunch, and I take a nap in the hammock Saturday afternoon and go to church with Steve, David, and their wives on Sunday. I plan to go to Sunday School with them, but David asks this important question, "Think about this. Between Sunday School and church, you will see lots of people who will want to see you and hug, etc. Do you want to do that?" Nope, I had not thought ahead to consider the logistics. So, I stay back at David's on Sunday morning, sitting on the front porch.

The peaceful, quiet, slow conversations with my brothers and their wives are a blessing. Someone mentioned yesterday that it is Mother's Day weekend; it takes me unaware. I realize that Steve and David made sure I had a plan for this emotional holiday, arriving on the heels of Jennifer's death.

Tuesday, May 14

I return to school on a day without students to complete end of the year paperwork. I start slowly; Emalie came to help me complete grades. Sadness did not show up while I work, but the concrete blocks come out tonight.

It just hurts too much to write in my journal.

Wednesday, May 15

When I call Donna, a friend who works at the Woodmont church, she says, "It's been a month." Even though I know this is true, saying it out loud puts it in front of me. I cry all day and much of the night.

Saturday, May 18

This chilly gray morning looks more like February than May, except the green trees and delicate purple iris blooms remind me May is Iris Month in Tennessee. Sitting on the deck I write my thoughts in a journal:

> *I miss her phone calls, our conversations about struggles, life, and her walk with you, Lord. I wonder about her conversations in Heaven. Are she and Mama exploring each other's lives? Do they sit with my grandmothers and their mothers to share memories? In this earthly body I can only relate to Heaven in these physical terms. Do they observe our daily struggles and see the whole picture as You do? Can they see where this journey leads me? Or is it nothing like that? Instead, is Heaven an ongoing praise of the Father, Son, and Spirit?*
>
> *What would Mama have said to Jennifer as she entered heaven? "Welcome home child. You have made the impact God wanted you to in only 21 years?" Did she introduce you to Grandmother Stephens and Mama Stephens? Did you suddenly see the big picture of your journey and where it began?*
>
> *Thank you, God, for quiet moments to meditate and create.*

All That Stuff

I make lists of her things that I can give away: clothes, books, childhood toys. Before Josh left for a trip out West I gave him her blue trunk full of books and memories. She first took that trunk to camp when she was a junior counselor and each year until she graduated from high school. It went to Tennessee Tech, and she covered it with pictures of all her trips and adventures. We gave Jennifer several of Max Lucado's books when she turned 18, so I gave them to Josh along with the Bible study book they studied together, her journals and keepsakes. We also give him Jennifer's mountain bike and gear as well as her winter skiing equipment.

The shelf of tiny animal families on her bedroom wall remind me of Brooke, Jennifer's best friend from preschool through high school. She and Brooke collected these families during their early years, playing together for hours, creating villages and homes out of scrap material and cardboard. I invite Brooke over to spend some time with me, going through all her childhood keepsakes. We pull out boxes and bags full of their childhood: notebooks, erasers, pens, and bookmarks of Hello Kitty. I encourage Brooke to take anything she wants; what will I do with this stuff? We will have no grandchildren; these memorabilia just remind me of the emptiness.

Her closet shelves are stuffed with notebooks from high school, notes, old tests. I pitch most of this while cleaning out her small closet. Courtney took most of the clothes in the early days after the funeral; I hope she can use them or give them to someone who will.

Reflecting on ways to keep Jennifer's memory alive, especially for her cousins and other family members, I begin making piles of Jennifer's books, jewelry, and stuffed animals. I set aside these items in groups for the cousins in Indiana and across Tennessee. A friend showed me a beautiful laminated bookmark made from the obituary of her son's death; I like this idea but replace the obituary with her picture and a significant Bible verse. This craft project engages a different part of my mind, and I quickly begin working at the computer.

My thoughts often return to the days before and after the funeral when so many gave flowers, food, time, money, and support. I try to write a few thank you notes each night.

*Jennifer's pre-school
picture at four years old*

*Larry, Martell, and Jennifer
when she was in 1st grade*

Monday, May 20

I stand in her doorway tonight. Time has stopped. Furniture from college is sitting in the middle of the room. Piles of books, stuffed animals, winter clothes, and all the things I can't seem to find a place for are scattered all over the room. "Where are you?" I whisper to myself. She can't be gone. I look at her picture from a trip to Gulf Shores just a few months ago and long to talk to her.

Tonight, Larry and I walk Jennifer's dog, Austin on our street. After several minutes of silence, he says, "I can't believe she is gone." It's been more than a month since her death, but we both wrestle with this new reality.

> *"Where is she, Lord? What is she doing now?"*
> *We never said good-by;*
> *a gaping hole of unfinished conversations remains.*

Before I go to sleep, I begin a letter to Jennifer, giving voice to the feelings and thoughts that fill my heart. (The letter follows this chapter)

Saturday, May 25

The First Wedding

Jennifer, Kim, Tracy, and Robin were in Color Guard together as eighth graders in the high school band. They remained close friends throughout high school. Kim's wedding is the first for the girls, and Jennifer was to be one of the bridesmaids.

Kim's wedding feels like another emotional hurdle to overcome. I mentally tell myself that our presence at the wedding is for Kim, knowing she is missing Jennifer as well. When we find our seat in the church, my eyes immediately focus on a candle burning on a table near the front of the auditorium. Kim told me some time before the wedding that she would use a candle to honor Jennifer.

Tears pour down my cheeks before the music begins. I can't seem to halt this waterfall of emotion. Tracy, Robin, and Melissa enter as bridesmaids, and I can't help but think of Jennifer. I weep through the whole service but want to stay afterwards to speak to Kim. Larry and I follow the other guests outside to a large tent set up with tables and chairs for the reception. We sit for a while waiting for the wedding party to finish with pictures inside. We don't see many people we know, which is fine with me because I don't want to talk. This weeping exhausts me, and my face shows it.

The longer we wait the more tense I feel. We talk for a few minutes to Tracy's mom and then we finally see Kim and her husband coming out of the church building. I give my congratulations, and Larry and I head for the car, escaping anymore encounters.

As we drive away, Larry asks me what I want to do, and I suggest we go see the new Spiderman movie. It is the perfect distraction to block out memories and sadness. And it was a good movie.

A reading in *My Utmost for His Highest* seems to be written just for me.

> *God is not concerned about our plans. He doesn't ask, "Do you want to go through this loss of a loved one, this difficulty, or this defeat?"*
>
> *The things that happen either make us evil, or they make us more saintly, depending entirely on our relationship with God and its level of intimacy.*[12]

Reading this entry, I think, "I don't want to be saintlier if it means losing my daughter."

This I Know Now

- My journal entries became heartfelt prayers:

> *This profound longing for the child and the woman who is gone burdens my soul. I just can't believe she is gone forever. My friend, my love, my daughter – how can it be?*

*Oh my God, do you hear my cry? Do you feel this ache,
this pain in my stomach?*

I ache for my mother AND my daughter.

*Jehovah Raphe, my healer. I claim your promise to heal my
soul of this pain. Heal Larry's heart, Lord. Give us what
we need in your time.*

*You gave us a blessing for 21 years. An unexpected gift,
and we delighted in her daily.*

- Laments in the Psalms expressed the rawness of my pain.

Psalm 3

*But thou O Lord, art a shield about me,
my glory and the lifter of my head. v. 3
I lie down and to sleep
I wake again,
for the Lord sustains me. v. 5 RSV*

- My newest understanding of this journey: EVERY day I must
take time to read, write, meditate, and pray as a physical,
mental, emotional, and spiritual process for grieving. Rather
than pushing aside thoughts or memories of Jennifer, I must
consciously consider them daily. If I don't, I hit these low
points with no warning. One author calls it, "leaning into the
pain". I write my feelings, prayers, scriptures, and insights in
my journals.
- Writing a letter to Jennifer provided a place for me to say all the
unsaid thoughts and feelings and a final goodbye.

Now I Am Thankful for:

- the respect and thoughtfulness of my students during seminar.
- family members who paid attention to my needs but did not
"hover"

- time with Brooke to process the passing of Jennifer's childhood

Your Turn:

- Don't worry about ANYTHING
- Pray about EVERYTHING, especially

- Tell God what I need
- Thank Him for all He has done.
- Perhaps writing a letter to God pouring out your pain, or a letter to your loved one who has died or to the person who betrayed/cheated/left you will give you some release in your heartache. Ask for his peace with confidence because I find guarding my heart and mind continues to help me on this journey.

Philippians 4:6-7

> *Then you will experience God's peace, which exceeds anything we can understand. His peace will guard your hearts and minds as you live in Christ Jesus. NLT*

LETTERS TO MY DAUGHTER

May 20, 2002

Dear Jennifer,

How full of life you were the last time we saw you! Wedding plans, summer plans, and your love for Josh were filling you up. Do you know how proud I am of you? Do you know that you blessed so many lives? You became a woman at college. You came so far from the teenager in high school who did not want Mama to interfere or <u>would not</u> believe me about some things. We had such good conversations – so much like those I had with my mother.

Do you know how much I love Josh? How pleased I was with your choice? As a couple, your devotion to God, your seeking hearts, your clear journey together on His path inspired and encouraged me.

May 22

Today I think of how you should be in Nashville, going to showers and teas for Kim, the first of your high school friends to get married. Josh was to come for the weekend, and no doubt you would need another fitting for your maid of honor dress. Instead, Kim will be remembering you at her wedding by lighting a candle. You would be packing your blue trunk as you and Josh head for Kamp Kanakuk for the summer. Of course, you always made a long list of things whenever you packed for trips.

Jennifer, you just blessed our lives every day! How thankful I am for your 21 years, the opportunities that you had to see the world and share the love of Jesus. The last five years of your life were just peak times for you in every area of your life. You were living that book that I wanted you to write for teenage girls about living healthy physically, spiritually. There could be no doubt in anyone's mind that healthy living, walking with God, and your love for Josh were intertwined into the fabric of your life. What a testimony!

May 25

How I missed you at Kim's wedding! She was beautiful, and the wedding was so sweet. Melissa looked great! I cried so much my sinuses were pounding.

But I don't feel you near. It feels like you are just away on another mission trip or at camp. Sometimes when I come home I think there will be a message from you on the answering machine, and I will be able to call you back to talk. Where are you?

I see you in Courtney and Kim, Brooke and Tracy, Daniel and Eric, Melissa and Stephanie. And especially Josh. To have you flop down on this bed and tell me about your day or chew on a problem – that is a joy to remember. A joy I will never experience again.

May 31

Jennifer, how brave you were! You faced your fears, your insecurities, with grace and charm, and you waded through. To think of you entering that high school in Cookeville to eat lunch with some of your teens from church reminds me of your days in ninth and tenth grades! How you struggled to seek out new friends, faced snobbery and hypocrisy, were lonely and even sad! You never whined and seldom complained.

You are a young woman frozen in time at the peak of beauty and holiness. What a time to go—perhaps at the pinnacle of your influence and example! Your decision to go to Tennessee Tech, instead of a college with many of your friends was courageous. It was another proud moment for me. God blessed your life, you blessed ours, and now – now – that card You pinned to your bulletin board years ago *(I am a citizen of heaven)* has come true.

Now, you truly are a citizen in heaven.

June 8

Last night as I prepared a Dutch apple pie, I thought of you: last Thanksgiving at Standing Stone State Park with all the relatives, you and Josh peeling apples for a pie. You delighted in your discovery of cooking and preparing foods for others to enjoy. Who would have thought, after several false starts that you would choose nutrition as a major? I suppose apple pies will always remind me of you.

How delightful for me to hear you tell about college experiences that took you back to our roots – to your grandmother and great-grandmother in the rhythm of their lives as homemakers – canning beans and tomatoes, making jelly and at the same time learning the science behind it all. You were challenged by it and relished it.

You are teaching us every day in small ways to appreciate every moment we live. Thank you, my child.

I will always love you,

Mom

Chapter 7
SEARCHING

"...the culture lies — you really do not get over the biggest losses.
You don't pass through grief in any organized way and it takes years
and infinitely more tears than people want to allow you.
Yet the gift of grief is so incalculable in giving you back to yourself."
—*Stitches*, Anne Lamott[13]

June 2002

Waves of grief sweep over me. How can I navigate through these treacherous waters without being sucked under?

My need to clarify, understand, and seek ways to cope feels like a compulsion. May and June, I search for resources to guide me through these dark days. I explore Scripture, especially <u>Psalms</u> and comb the local Christian bookstores to find writers that make sense to me (this was before bookstores were replaced with Amazon). Years ago, Helen Kubler-Ross' ground-breaking book on death, *On Death and Dying*[14] helped me as my father let go of this world. I gained several important insights into dying, and Charlie Walton's book helps, but I keep looking for more.

Psalm 42 expresses the desperate anguish of my soul, but when I discover *Mourning into Dancing* by Walter J. Wangerin I find a more complete understanding of the psalmist's grief. Wangerin's book enriches, enhances, and enlightens my knowledge of grief. My thirst for information turns me into a researcher as I highlight significant points and write quotes in my journal. The rich narratives of people in various stages of grief engage my interest. His writing requires reflection and rereading for me to totally comprehend the process of grieving.

This description of grief, "the knitting of wounded souls, the conjoining again of brokenness" soothes my weary soul.[15] This must be how God heals us – by putting a wounded soul back together, never again the same, but still, mended.

> When God heals our broken hearts,
> he puts a wounded soul back together,
> never the same, but still mended.

Stages of Grief

Since the publication of Kubler-Ross' book on the stages of grief, we now know that these stages don't begin at a specific time or have a clear ending, nor do they always occur in a specific order. Sometimes they even blend together.

Stage 1: Shock[16] or Silence[17]

Being overwhelmed is a common feeling in this early stage. A person might appear to handle a death just fine while in the stage of shock, even doing the right thing but feel nothing at all.

I recognize my emotions during the first two months are primarily in the stage of shock. It takes all my emotional forces to confront this death because of the strength of the pain, but numbing protects me, especially at first.

Stage 2: Fight[18] (Wangerin calls this fight "Wrestling with the Angel")

Www.goodtherapy.org calls this stage Victimhood: "a tug of war between a need to be safe and protect emotions AND the need to grow and confront traumatic memories." Each of us fights our battle with grief or trauma in different ways at different times, sometimes with our physical strength, sometimes with our heart, or sometimes with our intellect.

With all my strength I deny my loss in the early days of grief, I just can't believe it happened. This can apply to any loss, a death, a divorce, the loss of a job or a friendship.

With all my <u>heart</u> I fight against *what is* with rage, anger, or fury.

With all my <u>mind</u> I try to bargain with God by thinking or arguing death away, "If only things were different . . ."

Fighting is frequently displayed as denial. During the first night of Jennifer's death, Larry and I would wake up and say, "It's true; she's still dead." We were in shock and had to remind ourselves we weren't dreaming. And yet days and weeks after that we still say, "I can't believe she is gone."

Our mind plays such tricks on us because we want to believe so strongly that a mistake has been made. Sometimes when Larry and I pull in our driveway, for just a moment, I imagine checking the answering machine and hearing her voice. She will tell us that she has just been away.

Courtney, Jennifer's roommate, tells me about a horrible nightmare in which she dreamed Jennifer came into their apartment and told her she really had not died. The vivid dream woke her and left her with such a feeling of despair.

Denial takes a lot of work; it's a struggle to gain control when life is spiraling out of control. Many experts on grieving emphasize that there is no prescribed sequence for any of these stages. I find I can abandon one stage and move to another in a few days, only to return a month later to the one abandoned. Grieving keeps a heart unbalanced -- emotions can be hijacked with a song or by seeing an old friend.

Anger can appear in this stage, looking for someone to blame, looking for vengeance. In these first days of grief even though my pain is raw and intense, I have not felt anger.

Wangerin adds bargaining in this stage - a battle in the mind or intellect. I continually battle between my head and my heart. If I can completely comprehend this death, then I can control it, thus the continued reading and searching for answers in books and in Scripture. Wangerin also suggests that the griever struggles to identify the causes of the death, to learn the sequence of events that led to it, and then selects one detail to consider *what if.* Illogically, the mind fights for power over this death.

Act 3: Sadness Only or Survivorhood[19]

The worst moments of grief: hopelessness, despair, even surrender. This stage may feel like dying, like God is indifferent or absent. Wangerin describes continual crying as "eyes keep leaking."[20] I often used this phrase in my journals when I found myself weeping. It could happen at any moment, often taking me by surprise. Wangerin refers to "good grief" in the book, and near the end, he explains what it means. "The <u>goodness of grief</u> is that it dramatically sheers the self away."[21] Our façade of self-control, our belief that we are independent will finally be reduced until we are ready for Act 4.

Act 4: Acceptance[22] or Thriving and Transcendence

The griever slowly realizes that she is still living, there is a tomorrow, and the present moment is a gift. It is when I can feel healed and safe[23]; I'm not sure I can even imagine that day.

Trevecca

Just a few months before Jennifer died in April 2002, I began a three-year course of studies at Trevecca Nazarene University in Nashville to earn a doctorate in education. The uniqueness of the program comes in its cohort organization and the writing of the dissertation at the same time as courses are taken. Careful selection of students for each new class places them in groups of 25. Each cohort group remains together throughout the course of three years, every semester. As soon as a topic is approved, we begin writing Chapter One in the second semester. By April 2002, I was in the middle of writing the first chapter; after April 13, writing my dissertation became a life preserver I clutched like a person drowning.

This I Know Now:

- Reading and rereading, highlighting, and note taking Wangernin's book deepened my understanding of my feelings and prepared my expectations.

- One of the summer session assignments at Trevecca provided another piece of evidence of the importance of gratitude. I wrote the entries listed below.
- This psalm for this time:

Psalm 25:4-6

Lord, tell me your ways.
Show me how to live.
Guide me in your truth,
And teach me, my God, my Savior.
I trust you all day long.
Lord, remember your mercy and love
That you have shown since long ago. NCV

Now I Am Thankful for:

- these morning devotions, for new insights, comfort, encouragement, and time to think.
- God's Word, it's ever fresh and renewing power, for all those Bible heroes and their stories.
- all those who have ministered to Larry and me in the past few months – their kindness, compassion, caring, and concern. How could we have coped without them?
- the distractions of the University, for topics and books that engage my mind, especially for the ability to focus – You have heard my prayer and blessed me.

Your Turn:

- Don't worry about ANYTHING
- Pray about EVERYTHING

- Tell God what I NEED,
  not what I want
- THANK Him for all He has done.

Philippians 4:6-7

> *Then you will experience God's peace, which exceeds any-thing we can understand. His peace will guard your hearts and minds as you live in Christ Jesus. NLT*

PSALM 42 AND 43

*Grief is not an enemy. It is the hurt of healing.
Grief is the grace of God within us,
the natural process of recovery.*[24]

For many years I only knew Psalm 42 through a devotional song that popped up in the 1980s, often sung by teenagers. I can't remember studying the laments of the Psalms even though I had a class in college on the poetical books of the Bible. But after Jennifer's death Psalm 42 kept showing up in the books I read on grief and even in a new song by the Christian group, Zoe.

Since those early days of grief in 2002, I've poured over these verses and recently taught them in adult Bible classes. Nancy Guthrie's study *Seeing Jesus in the Psalms* provides a rich background for understanding laments and specifically Psalm 42 and 43.[25]

Perhaps the most enlightening thought I gained from Guthrie is this: these laments teach us to talk back to our God-doubting thoughts.[26] The words of this psalm often echoed my thoughts, doubts, and depression.

Over sixty-five laments found in Psalms follows this general pattern:[27]

- Addressing God
- Complaint
- Trust
- Request for deliverance or a reason for God to act
- Assurance
- Praise

The writer of Psalms 42 and 43 swings from faith to lament and back to faith over and over in his thoughts. Verses one through three introduce the psalmist's cry to God using the metaphor of a panting deer thirsting for a stream of water. The writer feels such a desperate isolation from God he is like an animal searching for water in a dry land, then he lays out his complaint in these verses.

As the deer longs for streams of water,
so I long for you, O God.
I thirst for God, the living God.
When can I go and stand before him?

Psalm 42:1,2

Day and night I have only tears for food,
while my enemies continually taunt me, saying,
"Where is this God of yours?"

Psalm 42:3 NLT

This longing for God can be related to Christ's isolation from God when He hung from the cross. He physically thirsted for water, just as His soul longed for the Father. He cried out on the cross, "My God, my God, why have you abandoned me?" (Mark 15:34). NLT

Have you felt abandoned by God? I did. I could swing from despair to hope just as easily as the psalmist. Knowing Jesus understands these feelings from His own experience gives me comfort. My suffering cannot compare to the crucifixion of Jesus, but knowing He suffered for me and my sins give me an anchor in the stormy waters of my sorrow.

Changing back to faith and trust, the writer remembers how he used to be a leader in the house of God singing for joy and celebrating God's goodness.

My heart is breaking
as I remember how it used to be:
I walked among the crowds of worshipers,
leading a great procession to the house of God,
singing for joy and giving thanks
amid the sound of a great celebration!

Psalm 42:4 NLT

Reminding ourselves of times of thanksgiving and celebration can replace the heartbreak. Therefore, the practice of giving daily thanks can actually transform a heart. Renewing our minds through God's Word, through memories of his blessings, and writing down his gifts can change the way we think. If I <u>believe</u> God has blessed me, I <u>feel</u> loved, treasured, and safe.

The chorus of this psalm (verses five and eleven) includes both lament (first two lines) and trust (next three lines) in the same verse. Is this not how our emotions work? This back and forth helped me know I wasn't losing my mind.

Why am I discouraged?
Why is my heart so sad?
I will put my hope in God!
I will praise him again –
my Savior and my God!

Psalm 42:5, 11 NLT

His lament returns again when he remembers God from the headwaters of the Jordan River and hears raging seas sweep over him. This ache in his soul feels like drowning, overwhelmed by the rushing water. I love the image used in the NIV for verse seven, "Deep calls to deep." In Randy Gill's song "Deep Calls to Deep" one line expresses this so well: "There is a time for sorrow when deep calls to deep."

Now I am deeply discouraged,
but I will remember you–
even from distant Mount Hermon,
the source of the Jordan,
from the land of Mount Mizar.
I hear the tumult of the raging seas
as your waves and surging tides
sweep over me

Psalm 42:6,7 NLT

Again, in a statement of faith and assurance, as if he can hear the Lord call him, the writer reminds himself of God's steadfast love in the next verse.

But each day the Lord pours
his unfailing love upon me,
and through each night
I sing his songs,
praying to God who gives me life.

Psalm 42:8 NLT

The complaint in this lament returns, questioning God and complaining about his enemies. Notice the enemies taunt him just as mockers taunted Jesus as he hung on the cross. "Those who passed by . . ." said, "He trusts in God. Let God rescue him now if he wants him, for he said, "I am the Son of God." (Matt. 27:39, 43) NCV

"O God my rock," I cry,
"Why have you forgotten me?
Why must I wander around in grief,
oppressed by my enemies?"
Their taunts break my bones.
They scoff, "Where is this God of yours?"

Psalm 42:9, 10 NLT

Psalm 42 ends with a repeat of the chorus of verse five and the last verse of Psalm 43 repeats the same questions "Why am I discouraged and sad?" and then preaches to himself "to put his hope in God!" (Psalm 42:5,11). Psalm 43 expands on the lament of the writer's circumstances in verses one and two while in verse three he asks God to lead him to the place where God dwells. Then he can offer a sacrifice of praise and worship.

Declare me innocent, O God!
Defend me against these ungodly people.
Rescue me from these unjust liars.
For you are God, my only safe haven.
Why have you tossed me aside?
Why must I wander around in grief?
oppressed by my enemies?

Send out your light and your truth;
let them guide me.
Let them lead me to your holy mountain,
to the place where you live.
There I will go to the altar of God,
to God – the source of all my joy.
I will praise you with my harp,
O God, my God!
Why am I discouraged?
Why is my heart so sad!
I will put my hope in God!
I will praise him again –
my Savior and my God!

Psalm 43:1-3 NLT

Guthrie's explanation of the laments helped me in the struggle between the heart and head by explaining that the psalms provide a vocabulary for our feelings, teaching me to talk back to those feelings that cause me to question God. She continues with this: when we think differently and believe differently, we begin to feel differently. Our emotions flow out of what we believe is true.[28]

Henry Nouwen's classic book, *Turning My Mourning into Dancing*, addresses our need to avoid suffering in today's culture; we consider it annoying! And I did exactly what he says many of us do, I tried to keep busy to escape the pain.[29]

Chapter 8
STARR MOUNTAIN

When the gift of Jennifer's life was snatched away,
I realized how great it was.
But the pain of no more outweighs the gratitude of the once was.
—Adapted from *Lament for a Son*

July 2002

After July 4, I pack suitcases and books to begin the summer session at Trevecca, living on campus for nine days. We live in the dorms and eat in the cafeteria, not so convenient or comfortable, but it does make it easier to focus on the task ahead. Days and evenings are filled with intense academic work, but I find healing in unexpected places.

In a course on leadership we read and practice *The Seven Habits of Highly Effective People* by Steven Covey. Our cohort bonds and grows stronger during these days by practicing the habits we learn, frequently affirming each other through notes and encouragement as we work on projects. I receive many supportive notes and words from my fellow students; their support comforts me throughout the week.

I keep the habit of journaling every morning, a requirement for one class. I find this habit essential in healing.

Saturday, July 6

First Day on Campus, Journal Entries

God gives us a vision – He is getting us into the shape of the goal He has for us."[30] I continue to wonder if Jennifer had completed her job on earth. Certainly, she had reached a pinnacle, but her potential to do more makes me question whether God's hand was in her death.

God, is your vision for me this path of grieving? I don't think so, but I know You expect me to use it to Your glory. Guide my feet, Lord.

Monday, July 8

These early mornings of intimate fellowship with the Father fill my spiritual bank account. During moments of crisis, I can withdraw what I need.

God, you are faithful and holy. You have blessed me with love and support through these difficult days. I praise you for Your abundance.

Saturday, July 9

One of our assignments in the doctoral program this week includes writing a mission statement and creating an action plan for our lives. This plan must include all dimensions of life – physical, emotional, intellectual, spiritual. We make our presentations on the last day of class; when we meet again this fall we report on our progress. Explaining my Personal Plan for Life in a PowerPoint presentation in front of professors and fellow cohort members commits me and holds me accountable.

For my beginning slide I quoted from Oswald Chamber's writings in *My Utmost for His Highest:*

"'The clouds are the dust of His feet.' Nahum 1:3 NIV

...sorrow, bereavement, and suffering are actually the clouds that come along with God! He does not come in clear-shining brightness.

He does not want to teach us something in our trials. . ..

*He wants us to **unlearn** something.*

His purpose in using the cloud is to simplify our beliefs until our relationship with Him is like a child. . ."[31]

My plan for physical improvement includes yoga and swimming; for spiritual growth, I plan to continue daily prayer, meditation, and journaling. The path ahead for emotional well-being is not so clear; grief overwhelms me so easily, but I do have a next step which includes Larry. We will climb the same mountain Jennifer and Josh did and see the place where she left this world.

After the summer session at Trevecca, Larry and I plan to meet Josh and his family at their cabin outside Cleveland, Tennessee. Jennifer and Josh drove a few miles from the family cabin to the Cherokee National Forest and Starr Mountain where they hiked on the day of her death. We want to hike that trail; we need to see the place where she died.

Even though Josh described the place, Larry and I both need a picture in our heads of where her life ended. I can't remember which one of us suggested this trip, but both of us believe this is our "next step." After my presentation, classmates and friends question us about making this pilgrimage, but something pulls the two of us, as well as Josh's family, back to this place.

Once classes end on July 13, I'm sleep deprived, emotionally drained, cognitively stimulated, spiritually uplifted. I don't know how I could have made these last nine days without the support of my cohort group.

Friday, July 19

Journal Entry

The Lord is my shepherd; I have everything I need.

Psalm 23:1 NIV

I know the Lord is guiding me through this dark valley. He is watching over me and waiting patiently for me to follow.

Lord, I know You held Jennifer in the palm of Your hand when she died, and she is with you now.

This beautiful July morning reminds me of how carefully God created this world. A gentle breeze moves the dark green leaves of the tulip poplar; birds and insects sing around me, and sunlight creates shadows on the fence. God is so good!

Friday afternoon Larry and I drive south to the cabin to stay with Josh's family. We hug each other in a joyful reunion and tour their beautiful log home, just as Jennifer described it.

Saturday, July 20

After breakfast Saturday morning, we ride with Josh's parents (Jan and Debbie), his sister, Katie, and Josh to Starr Mountain. We drive down a dusty gravel road and park beside a nearly dry Gee Creek. Only a few cars line the roadside as hikers prepare to climb. First, we decide to climb to the point where Jennifer fell – near the top of Starr Mountain.

The mountains around us are lush with the summer blend of greens from pine, maple, oak, hickory, and locust trees. Josh told us that this was a rough trail, but the steepness surprises us. The undergrowth of the forest closes around us as we follow a bare earthen path. I find myself quickly out of breath and struggling to climb. When I look up the path, I see no level places, just big tree roots, rocks, and boulders. We grab the roots to keep steady and pull ourselves up. This straight-up trail has no switchbacks. Josh and Katie, seasoned climbers, easily outdistance the four parents and wait for us to catch up.

As our group of four parents struggle up the trail, I thought how easily Jennifer could climb this trail. She maintained her physical fitness even after she quit the track team. Josh comments, "She sometimes sprinted up climbs such as this."

The trail changes from dirt to rock ledges and larger and larger boulders.

71

Starr Mountain, view from below. Jennifer fell from the cliffs near the top.

At one point we encounter a group of kids with a leader teaching a lesson on "Jesus is our rock." We wait for them to finish since the boulders are now cliffs and sheer walls. The ridgeline finally provides a level stone path, taking us under a ledge, around layers of rock and through an impossibly narrow passage before we finally reach the trail at the top of the cliffs. We still have not reached the top of the mountain. The trees thin out below us, but one lone stunted pine somehow grows straight out of rock and now leans into the outcropping of boulders.

Josh shows us the spot where Jennifer fell. The only way forward requires a hiker to cross a wide gap in the cliff. The expanse is too dangerous and too wide to leap across, but a narrow triangle of rock juts out between the two sides of the cliff. Sitting on this triangle provides the safest way to cross the expanse. A hiker with one foot on the large boulder to the right and the other on the boulder to the left swivel over to the other side.

Jennifer, Josh, and Katie crossed this place on their way up to the summit. When they started down, Jennifer ran ahead of Josh and Katie. When she sat on the rock, she lost her balance and had nothing to grasp to break her fall.

We immediately notice the steel cable placed in the wall of the cliff. Since Jennifer's death, Josh's parents lobbied the national park staff constantly to make this spot safer. Much to their surprise, a cable is attached to the cliff in the exact spot where Jennifer needed something to grab.

Once we stand on the ledge next to the triangle of the boulder I understand how this accident could occur. The danger here almost takes my breath away. Larry grabs the cable and stands in the same place she stood and leans over the edge. She had to sit on the point of the ledge and pivot her feet around to the other side. Because Jennifer ran ahead of Josh and Katie, no one was there to steady her. If only the cable had been there . . ..

I'm not afraid of heights, but I get a bit dizzy looking down from heights. As I approach the edge, I feel a sudden need to sit down, but I decide its safer to lay down on my stomach and look over the ledge. It looks to me as though Jennifer would have landed on the rocks below, but Josh says her body went farther out and landed in the underbrush.

Larry and Jan walk across the point to look out over the whole valley, but

Josh does not cross over. We ask Josh and Katie questions to fill in more details of the accident. Josh takes dozens of pictures of the view, the cable, us, and the view down the sheer cliff.

What a peaceful, sweeping vista! We stay long enough to appreciate God's creation in this memorable place. The view across the mountains changes from rich dark green created by cloud shadows, to brighter green in brilliant sunshine, then to the next layer of blue-green, then soft blue that gives the smoky label to the Great Smoky Mountains.

We walk back down the trail as Josh and Katy try to locate the exact place they found Jennifer. No path leads to the place where her life ended. As we leave the path, we walk almost sideways to get through thick undergrowth and trees. Josh shows us the places where he jumped from boulder to boulder trying to reach her; he could easily have broken a leg. He describes again what a difficult time the rescuers had climbing up to them. Katie and Josh had to clear brush and undergrowth to make a path for rescuers wearing heavy protective gear while carrying a stretcher. I now carry a picture in my head of these rescuers carrying Jennifer down the mountain on the stretcher. I recognize the enormous difficulty of the task.

Josh locates the spot at the base of huge rock where he thinks she landed. We plant a lily in the ground that Debbie brought, then Josh prays and talks about the spot where Jennifer met God. After we climb down the mountain, we drive to the other side of the river to take a picture of the cliff face.

Climbing the mountain released a knot of pain and completed one piece of unfinished business in my grief. Josh says he could not have gone back up that mountain without us. Larry and I head back to Nashville late Saturday afternoon and attended church Sunday morning in Madison.

This I Know Now:

Making the journey together provided support for each of us in this group.

*Starr Mountain,
view from the
fall site.*

*Looking down
from the fall site.
Katie, Josh's sister
is lying on rock
ledge.*

Closure comes in many ways and at various times; this experience did not end my questions, but it did give me some peace.

I expected more emotions from at least some of us on the climb, but perhaps the focus on the physical struggle to climb diverted our emotions, giving us time for introspection.

The Seslers welcomed us to their home in this beautiful setting, giving me pictures of Jennifer's visit with them.

This verse in Isaiah sticks with me and I print it on a card to view on my desk.

Good people are taken away,
but no one understands.
Those who do right are being taken away
from evil and are given peace.
Those who live as God wants
find rest in death.

Isaiah 57: 1,2 NCV

Now I Am Thankful for:

- Jennifer's time on earth—a blessing to so many, and that her story continues to spread.
- God's peace I experienced which exceeds anything I can understand. I know it guards my heart and mind. (Phil. 4:7)
- all those who hold us up in prayer.

Your Turn:

- Don't worry about ANYTHING
- Pray about EVERYTHING
- Tell God what I NEED
- THANK Him for all He has done.

- In my circumstance today, I may not be able to see His gifts and blessings, but I can find at least three blessings today.

_____

_____

_____

Philippians 4:6-7

Then you will experience God's peace, which exceeds anything we can understand. His peace will guard your hearts and minds as you live in Christ Jesus. NLT

Chapter 9
LAMENT

*Telling others about our journey is harder
than actually making the climb.*

Saturday, July 27, 2002

Why didn't the climb up Starr Mountain grab my heart and wring it out? Why didn't I feel the heavy concrete blocks on my chest? Standing at the edge of the precipice where Jennifer lost her balance, where were my tears?

Perhaps my head distracted my heart with details of the trip. Once Larry and I committed to the trip, we had no second thoughts. I publicly committed to the journey in my last presentation at Trevecca.

But when we arrive home, the tears begin.

Sunday, July 28

Journal Entry

> *Now that it is done (the hike up the mountain), I've been "leaky" – last night and today.*
>
> *Today, the Lord's Day, I ask God to shield me from the depressing pain that threatens to overwhelm my soul --- I know this grief will remain. How can it not?*

This psalm of David's eloquently depicts the state of my broken heart.

Psalm 31:8-10

Lord, have mercy because I am in misery.
My eyes are weak from so much crying,
and my whole being is tired from so much grief.
My life is ending in sadness,
and my years are spent in crying.
My troubles are using up my strength,
and my bones are getting weaker.
But you heard my prayer when
I cried out to you for help.
All you who put your hope in the Lord,
be strong and brave.
NCV

Monday, July 29

Emalie comes over, and I share Josh's pictures of our climb. As soon as I begin talking about our trip I choke up with emotions and tears. The visit to Starr Mountain made everything fresh again. Being in Josh's home, eating meals with his family, swimming in the river, those experiences remind me she will never visit the cabin or his family again.

Tuesday, July 30

Journal Entry

Last night was for weeping and now I can't bear to look at pictures of Jennifer and Josh, full of life and joy. Doing anything in these moments is almost impossible. The gratitude journal I started this summer makes me weep; prayer makes me weep.

But here is a mystery-- one day can end in despair, and the next morning I awaken with hope and expectation. One day I cannot look at her pictures, and the next day I can put her pictures in an album without a heavy heart. I don't understand this.

All I know is that I <u>can</u> abide in the love of Christ. I <u>can</u> remember His peace and find comfort in His presence. I <u>know</u> He was with us as we climbed that trail and looked over the sweeping vistas of dark green valleys and smoky mountains.

Seeking

I remember a quote Dan Dozier used in Jennifer's funeral:

"Faith is a footbridge you can't know will hold you up over the chasm until you are forced to walk out on it." [32]

I search in bookstores for the book, *Lament for a Son*, and finally, find a thin paperback with short one-page laments. This little book expresses powerful emotions that find a connection to my heart. Nicholas Wolterstorff's son also died in a hiking accident in the mountains.

The writer provides me new insights into a familiar Scripture, Psalm 42. He compares the psalmist's faith to the tension of wood and string on a bow. The back and forth of the lament reveals a bruised faith, a longing faith, and a faith emptied of nearness. I turn the page and find these words describing my own despair, "I know now about helplessness – of what to do when there is nothing to do." [33]

The brief laments, filled with questions and expressions of pain, echo in my aching heart. So many of his laments express my unspoken cries. In the following quotes, I've replaced his references to his son with references to Jennifer.

"There's a hole in the world now. In the place where Jennifer was, there's now just nothing …Never again will anyone inhabit the world the way she did…The world is emptier. My daughter is gone. Only a hole remains, a void, a gap, never to be filled." [34]

"One small misstep and now this endless neverness." [35]

"I lament all that might have been and now will never be."[36]

Sundays

Exhaustive sorrow envelopes Sundays like a gray fog. I should just welcome this uninvited guest and accept its presence. Heartache comes and goes all day.

Going to church continues to be one of the hardest times of the week. As I sit in worship with Larry my throat tightens as an aching pain builds and builds. It will pour out in tears and sobs if I can't control it. Sobbing in church is not acceptable to me.

In these moments I don't want attention. So many sweet friends at church want to speak to me, tell me they are praying for me, but I can't even talk with this huge lump in my throat. I need to get away. Once I am safely home, fatigue sets in, and I'm in the recliner or on the couch for hours.

I talk to my brother, David, about my battle with Sundays; he works as a counselor in West Tennessee and is my occasional counselor. He sent me this email:

July 2002

Sis,

It is amazing how many times I hear people say how hard it is to go to church. "I'm doing fine all week long, but then on Sunday's, I slide back into the dark hole," or similar statements. My conclusion about that phenomenon is this: we keep our defense mechanisms in place during the week to function in our various roles (work, student, etc.), but on Sunday we let all those defenses relax, as we let our spirits and emotions go. In worship we are very introspective and open a part of us that is intensely intimate. But that opens the floodgates for every emotion we've been holding in check all week.

What I'm saying is that what is happening to you is normal.

For a while, you may occasionally have to sneak into worship at the last minute and leave before dismissal, or you may have to stay home occasionally. Your damaged spirit will need some time to heal itself.

Hope this is helpful.

David

His advice makes sense. Larry and I begin sitting in the very back of the church, which is no hardship for Larry since he prefers to sit in the back. We often leave before the last "Amen" to avoid the crowd. Larry is learning to read my emotions well; if something has opened my wounds during a service, he looks at me and whispers "Do we need to go?"

If I nod "yes", we leave. No questions, no discussion. I have no need to "talk about" this, and he understands. My emotions are sitting on the outside of my heart, and I just need some time alone.

Kindness of Strangers and Friends

Courtney comes by one afternoon with some library books Jennifer had checked out at the public library in Nashville. These are long overdue, and I had no idea the books even existed.

I drop them by the Madison branch of the library and explain the circumstances of the books. The clerk grabs my hands and says, "Don't worry about this. We'll take care of it." Tears well up in my eyes from the unexpected compassion she shows me.

On days without anguish, I find I can work on a project of memories. I gather all the comment sheets from the funeral, letters, copies of newspaper articles, and the memories written by the teens and college friends in Cookeville and put them in a book. I make a copy for us, one for Josh, and one for his family. I take one of the copies to Kinkos to get it bound. A young man waits on me; I tell him how I want it bound. I wait as he searches for a wire coil, then watch him punch holes and insert the coil. He presents the finished book to me, looks up and says, "No charge." His kindness touches me, and I try to hold back tears as I thank him.

A card comes in the mail from Vonda D., Jennifer's third-grade teacher. Jennifer had such a great year with her, loved the projects, bloomed as her confidence grew each day. Vonda remembers Jennifer well and I am touched by her kindness. Lauren, one of Jennifer's friends from high school, was her student teacher when Jennifer died.

As July is ending my thoughts lead me to the beginning of school. I drive to my middle school one morning to see if I can get in my room to begin arranging furniture. I stop by Rob's office, my principal. "Do you know you are a role model for people?" he asked. I shrug, can't think of a response. Later, reflecting on this exchange, I realize that I don't want that honor. I'd rather have my daughter back!

Another Mystery

One of my new routines takes me to a nearby indoor pool in the mornings to swim laps. After the swim I find a quiet bench near a pond to meditate and pray. With a long exhale I still my thoughts, close my eyes and wait. My thoughts drift again and again.

Suddenly, Jennifer appears, standing next to the throne of God, watching and realizing my struggles with concentration. She leans over and addresses the Father, "My mom could use a little help right now." My Abba in heaven reaches down and touches me on the shoulder. Tears of grief and joy stream down my face. To see my daughter in heaven brings such joy but my aching soul finds healing in the love of a Father who knows my pain.

How can I explain this vision? Was it just my imagination? Neither matters to me. My heart-deep sorrow finds solace, and I hide this memory like a treasure in my heart.

Lately, my grief feels like Wangerin's "Act 3 of Grief."[37] He says part of this act is about dying yourself. Then a passage from another book comes to mind.

Reeve Lindbergh, daughter of Charles Lindbergh and Anne Morrow Lindbergh, kept a journal about her mother's last days, *No More Words*. The Lindberghs suffered a public kidnapping and murder of their firstborn child in 1932. When Reeve's first son died before he was two years old, she recalls this conversation with her mother:

"At the time of my son's death, when I asked my mother what would happen to me as the mother of the child, how that part of me would continue, she said, 'It doesn't. You die, that's all. That part of you dies with him. And then amazingly, you are reborn.'"[38]

Wednesday, July 31

The first week of every August I join many other teachers in preparing our classrooms for students. This pre-service work does not earn us any money, but these days are the only time to arrange furniture and supplies, as well as decorate bulletin boards since all the in-service days are filled with meetings. It helps to get a head start on the organizing.

After a hard day of unpacking boxes, sorting through files, and arranging furniture in my classroom, I attend a Wednesday night class that focuses primarily on worship songs. I don't have the energy to sing, so I just listen to the songs of praise. Music pours over me like waves of grief pouring over my soul. When "Surround Us O Lord" begins, my tears flow; this song brings back memories of the first night of Jennifer's death. I slip out the back during the last song, so I do not have to greet friends.

Thursday, August 1

Journal Entries

> *Lord, hold me close as these days become busy. I covet this quiet time each day and need the calming and slowing down. I need to pull within and restore my soul each morning. These past three months have established a practice of communing with You, God. I can feel its healing power.*

Sunday, August 4

Last night, a time to weep with gut-wrenching sobs. Just when I think I am doing well, the bottom falls out. Looking at her picture, I ask God, "Where is she?" Sometimes she seems lost, just a name, not the vibrant joyful person we knew. She is truly frozen in time at the peak of her beauty, energy, fitness, love, and life. Her future looked so bright and full of potential.

Even though August is my busiest time of the year, Jennifer and I still had time for long conversations as she shared her adventures and plans. While I worked on my classroom she spent her days cleaning out her blue trunk, washing clothes, shopping, and packing to return to school. Precious memories of precious times.

Grief and mourning have changed me. Why did she have to die?

These days make me think of Courtney, alone in their apartment, and I wonder how she copes with the grief? Getting up every morning and going to work, that's how I cope. Perhaps I should give her a call this weekend.

Tuesday, August 6

Prayer in Journal

> *Jehovah Raphe, my Healer, I need your healing power as I minister to my students. I cannot do this alone. My grief is too close to the surface and only You can heal my wounds. I turn this over to You Lord.*
>
> *As I begin the school year officially tomorrow I have lost some of my zeal and energy. I will need your hand, Father, to hold me up as I become tired or sad.*
>
> *I place my teaching goals for this school year before You:*

- To give my moments to You
- To pray for my students
- To remember my mission statement – a Spirit-filled center
- To do less and accomplish more by slowing down.

> *Father, I pray that You give me the power and strength physically, spiritually, emotionally, and cognitively to do these things.*

Thursday, Aug. 8

Journal Entry

> *When a person is drowning, the rescuer asks her to let go, to become helpless, so the rescuer can take over. God is my Rescuer, and I must become helpless and powerless. How often have I relied on myself? Too many times. Hard lessons to learn – trust, empty me.*
>
> *Father, You are holy. I am unworthy.*

Saturday, Aug. 10

As the week ends, I feel the answer to Tuesday's prayer: strength to complete my tasks. Desks arranged, supplies organized, bulletin boards completed, and time to slow down. I even help two team members finish their classrooms.

This morning's meditation says, "God places His saints where they will bring the most glory to Him and we are totally incapable of judging where that may be."[39]

Saints don't know where they can bring God the most glory. I think of the places where Jennifer served God and know she gave Him glory in unlikely places. Her decision to leave the Tennessee Tech track team and give up her scholarship was shared in the school's newspaper after her death. She believed her place that junior year was with the teenagers at Collegeside church, a place where His glory touched many teenagers.

Every day this week was filled with busy-ness, but every night ended with tears and anguish. Last night I felt flat --- sad, sad.

My Support Team

Seeing friends, co-workers, and administrators at school this week reminds me of how supportive they were during the final months of last year. So many of the faculty and staff attended Jennifer's funeral.

Earlier in the week, Rob asks me if I want him to say something to the faculty to avoid the attention and hugs. What will be best for me? I understand people want to show their compassion; I've given many hugs to some of these people in their time of need. It seems easier to just let things happen naturally.

My greatest support comes from my team of eighth-grade teachers. Just as Larry helps me cope by not hovering or questioning, by just being there, these good friends do the same every day. Sometimes I use Emalie's line, "Don't be nice to me. It makes me cry."

Diane, one of our school counselors, tells me to come to her office anytime I need to get away or cry in private. What a great offer, but I don't expect to need it.

Preparing My Heart and Mind for Students

Anticipating students' arrival, a passage from *God Calling* resonates with me: "Let nothing that others do to you alter your treatment of them."[40] What powerful words! I need to practice this over and over. Eighth graders emotions sometimes change from moment to moment, altering the classroom dynamics in an instant.

The research for my dissertation on critical thinking, writing, and character led me to an author with a unique point of view regarding the character of students. Michael Loehrer[41] believes a crisis in the classroom provides an opportunity to give a transfusion to a student who is bleeding internally. Past experiences bring up the image of an angry student, lashing out like a wounded animal, except her bleeding is inside.

During a crisis, if I can treat students with love and consideration just as Jesus would, the moment becomes an opportunity to instill a transfusion of virtue. I am mindful of the need for a sweetness of spirit and compassion for my students who are bleeding inside.

I Wish I Had Known Then

about surrender and sitting with sadness. Greenspan provides three skills she calls Emotional Flow, one of which is surrender. She advises, "To let it go, you have to let it flow."[42] Instead of trying to escape the pain of grief, surrendering to the sadness is a form of sincere acceptance. I know surrender takes time, but this language and learning to "sit with my sadness" could have given me more context. I slowly learned I had to go through the pain, not avoid it, but my stubborn heart struggled against it for a long time.

Now I Am Thankful for:

- the kindness of strangers
- books telling the stories of the author's journey into grief
- my support team at school
- Larry's understanding of my needs

Your Turn:

- Don't worry about ANYTHING, even

  _____

- Pray about EVERYTHING
- Tell God what I need
- Thank Him for all He has done.

Philippians 4:6-7

> *Then you will experience God's peace, which exceeds anything we can understand. His peace will guard your hearts and minds as you live in Christ Jesus. NLT*

Chapter 10
MOURNING

Thank you, God, for days I am not in the pit.

Friday, August 9

Leaving school this afternoon I could feel the dark cloud of sorrow coming. I continue to swing from despair to hope, back to despair as school begins, which means I remain in Sadness of Act 3[43]. Truly finding the Acceptance of Act 4 seems a long time coming.

Tonight we celebrate our thirty-third anniversary, so our plans distracted me from my depression. We change clothes and drive downtown to eat at one of the more expensive restaurants on Broadway, Merchant's Restaurant.

Saturday, despair returns along with exhausting tears. Thankfully, Larry continues to support me and gives me what I need during these times.

During the first week of school, I talk to my classes about making a difference in the lives of others during their eighth-grade year, briefly discussing Jennifer and how she impacted many lives. I have not shared details about her death; before telling them that story I must determine if I am able to talk about it.

Deep Mourning

Sunday, August 18

A deep-seated heaviness lingers, emerging each weekend; I have more time to think and remember when I am not teaching. It has been four months since Jennifer died; even though she spent many weeks in the summers at camp and mission trips, we have never been apart this long. During her last year at Tech, she came home several times a semester – that feels like a lifetime ago.

Friday, August 30

Two encounters this week with students provide opportunities of crisis. Brittany P. loudly demands, "How can I get my schedule changed?"

"Which class do you want to change?" I ask.

"Yours. You're the only teacher I have a problem with."

"What is the problem?"

She lists a few: dress code, no textbook. I ask her to step to the hall, so we can talk privately. After a few interruptions, which leave her waiting (perhaps stewing), I finally face her and request that she listen first. She crosses her arms and frowns.

"Listen to the question I asked you earlier. 'Did you do any of the home-work?' Not 'did you do it all? Or do you have a textbook?'" She actually listens! I ask which day she finally received her textbook and suggest she do as much of the assignment as she can by Tuesday.

She lets out a heavy sigh and agrees. This girl wears anger like a suit of armor, but I'm sure she is "bleeding inside." I feel some satisfaction that she listened, and her momentary frustration appears to dissipate.

The second incident begins when Jaime F. comes into class after the late bell. Her puffy eyes, splotchy skin, and smeared mascara reveal something is wrong; I take her to the hall (my private conference room). Her sister (a former student) is scheduled for surgery today, and Jaime has not heard from anyone. Tears begin spilling down her cheeks. I rein in my first impulse to downplay the situation; drama frequently shows up in encounters with this family.

I suggest that surgery could have started late. "Take a deep breath, think good thoughts, pray, and wait a little longer," I advise.

"Can I call at lunch?" she asks; I give her permission. When I see her later in the day, she tells me surgery was delayed. Her big smile indicates her relief.

We hug, and I question, "Was I right?"

She shrugs, grins, and grudgingly admits, "Yes".

A third encounter surprises me when I stop for groceries at Kroger. A former student, now in high school, bags my groceries and tells me he is sorry about my daughter. His compassionate response is unexpected, so out-of-character for him. As soon as I reach the car the tears begin and continue all the way home. Weariness puts down roots and stays while Larry helps me unload groceries. Later, I sit on the deck to think. How lonely the days are without her. I just wish I could talk to her and see her face. It still seems impossible that she is not here anymore.

On Sunday I plan to drive up to Mayme's (Mama's sister) in Kentucky for Labor Day weekend. My cousin, Rene, will be there. Since Mama's death her older sister, Mayme, has been a source of wisdom and strength for me. I am eager to see her since she was unable to come to the funeral; a visit with her connects me to my roots.

Tuesday, September 3

The visit with Mayme and Rene includes plenty of laughter while reliving the funeral brings tears. It was good to be there, remembering the summers of my childhood. I leave a funeral video, but I have not watched it, have no desire to see it. The pain remains much too strong.

Sorrow returns last night after talking to Courtney. When that despondency seeps into my soul, I don't care about anything.

Wednesday, September 4

I decide to inform my students of my plan in case on any given day I cannot continue teaching because of my emotions. I explain that I will write a message on the board describing the situation along with an assignment in the textbook. That way I will not have to leave the room but can sit at my desk (something I seldom do) while they work. I expect them to do this without questions since talking is the last thing I want to do. Feelings begin building inside me fourth period when I explain the plan but am able to finish. When emotions begin welling up with heaviness in my chest, I know I cannot continue talking. I hope I don't have to use this plan but being prepared makes us all feel better. Each class listens respectfully and have no comments or questions.

Yesterday after school, the familiar depression returns when I get in my car; I have difficulty breathing when it happens. Josh called last night; he has been very busy with his research and classes – keeping late hours to get the work done. We talk about our struggles. He wonders where she is right now – asleep in Paradise or in Heaven. I tell him about my experience trying to meditate by the pond and seeing her in heaven. This seems to help him.

After his phone call, I feel the pain fresh again and cry profusely. I don't fall asleep for a long time.

Saturday, September 7

Yesterday two scrapbooks arrived in the mail from Liz, a counselor Jennifer worked with at Kamp Kanakuk. One book is for Josh, and one for us. Each book is filled with pictures and letters from the campers who lived in Liz, Jennifer, and Danielle's cabin last summer. So many memories and so many people who loved her. What a joy to see the sweet letters from her campers!

I still question "Why, God?" Wasn't there so much more she could have done?

Wednesday, September 11

Last September 11th found our faculty in a meeting before school; when we heard about the first plane crash, we rushed to turn on televisions in our classrooms before students arrived on buses. When the second plane hit the World Trade Center, most students and teachers in our school were watching. The memory of last year's tragedy in New York, the Pentagon, and Pennsylvania is fresh on everyone's mind today. The grief of all the families who lost someone on a plane, in the towers, the Pentagon, or rescuing others opens the wounds of my broken heart.

At lunch Michelle, my next-door teacher, tells me about Brittany P.'s comments on courage. This is her definition of courage: "What Mrs. Souder's going through! That's courage. We don't know those other people in New York, but she's right here."

Just when I think a student is impossible to teach or is too disruptive, she shows her true character. I can't help but think our earlier encounter influenced Brittany's feelings. Teaching eighth-graders always challenges, often frustrates, sometimes surprises and occasionally inspires.

I choose not to go to church tonight; I want to be part of the service but feel sure emotions would swamp my tender heart.

Weekend of September 22

Saturday, Larry and I eat lunch with Josh and friends. He comes to church with us on Sunday, and a different group of friends meets us for lunch at a Mexican restaurant. I do my best to hide my pain.

After he leaves, an abyss of grief holds on all afternoon and into the evening. It remains Monday morning and continues after school. Larry leaves for Miami tomorrow to work on a video production.

During the school day, I can push away the grief, but the necessary early morning soul-work I established this summer has gradually disappeared. Until my ear infection clears up, no swimming is allowed.

Sunday, October 6

The first class of the new semester at Trevecca began this weekend. One year ago, another cohort member, Polly, experienced the death of her 21-year-old son. She says her grief just gets worse; even though we are not close friends, it helps to share our journeys each time our class meets.

My research proposal still awaits the approval of my school system. I need to begin the active research portion of my dissertation soon but must have approval from the school board. Anxiety lurks beneath the surface of Trevecca waters while I study for exams, complete class projects, and continue my research.

As the six-month anniversary date of Jennifer's death nears, desolate days alternate with drifting; numbness is a blessing. A friend at church asks me if I have considered taking something for the depression. I take so much medication now for my allergies, high cholesterol, and blood pressure; I am reluctant to add another pill to the pile. My darkest periods of desolation have not lasted more than two days; just when gut-wrenching pain pulls me toward a dangerous undertow, a new morning surfaces with hope. I don't welcome these times, but I expect them. I <u>should</u> feel sad that Jennifer is gone.

I haven't talked to Josh since he was here in September. I think maybe it is too hard for him to talk to us– his pain is obvious. He and Courtney both are suffering, and I'm not sure I am any help.

A Plea for Help

> Lord, please hold us all up in our grief and let us feel your strong power and grace.
>
> You hold me up through despair and grief. Six months of this pain feels like a lifetime. It still does not seem real.
>
> God, you are my Healer, and I cry out to You from the depths of my soul. When will the pain and despair ease? I ache for that last reunion with all the redeemed who have gone before me.
>
> I seek an answer to my research project and how to proceed.

Hitting a Wall

Jennifer's birthday comes soon, November 17; Thanksgiving, and Christmas holidays loom ahead, and I know they hold land mines for me.

Every day I walk through fields of landmines buried beneath the surface, an unknown number of explosive devices await a misstep. Some days I remember to tread carefully, but on other days I totally forget and walk through dangerous fields. When a memory explodes in my face, sorrow and despair shock my unsuspecting heart.

Friday, November 1

Time for meditation or journaling still escapes me, and I feel the effects. Still no word about my research proposal. I'm beginning to wonder what I can do with only one semester left in the school year.

Jennifer's room remains untouched in the last four months. When I stop in her doorway, I say over and over, "She's not here anymore."

Tuesday, November 12

Pushing away my grief by not having quiet moments leaves me unprepared for the coming holidays. They loom like storm clouds. Her birthday is Sunday, and I don't know how to spend that day.

Deadlines at Trevecca press on me, and my evenings are full of research and study. But some nights I just lie on the couch and watch TV. I had a great visit with family this weekend at Steve's (brother living in Henderson), but I still avoid church and emotional moments. If only summer mornings could appear, so I would have time to pray and meditate.

Friday, November 15

All day feelings of grief and pain sweep over me. During the school day, I feel weepy and fatigued. Teacher friends talk me into meeting at Famous Dave's Restaurant after school, and I go but feel alone and sad in the midst of a crowd.

Larry and I meet at another restaurant for dinner. Anything to distract me from moments of pain. Courtney calls when we get home and reminds me of the Bridal Tea for her on Saturday. I had forgotten this invitation; she really wants me to come. Thinking of Jennifer's friends reminds me of my loss. How I miss her!

Saturday, November 16

The morning mail contains a beautiful card from Josh's mother, with sweet words about Jennifer. One of the teachers at school is expecting the birth of his baby on the eighth of November, the day after her birthday. It's just not fair.

If Courtney had not asked me to come to her tea, I would have left when the first tears fell. I wish for Courtney's sake that Jennifer had been there for her; they were so close, and I know Courtney felt supported by Jennifer. I hold myself together as long as I can and then Courtney walks out with me to my car.

When I get home, I build a fire and wallow in misery for the rest of the day.

Sunday, November 17

We go to Woodmont Hills church on the other side of town today, again looking for distractions. We visit one of my favorite bookstores afterward and then meet friends for lunch.

Josh calls tonight; he says he cried all during church. I am okay all afternoon, but depression sets in at bedtime.

Monday, November 18

When the alarm goes off, fatigue and grief overwhelm me. Getting out bed feels like climbing a mountain. But I know I must go to school today; four of the teachers on our team will be absent. Getting ready requires concentration because I have no energy. Before my first class arrives, I write this message on the board:

"Yesterday was Jennifer's birthday. Please work on this assignment:"

I try not to exert any energy; exhaustion follows every footstep. When we take our lunch break, tears run down my face as I walk to the teachers' lunchroom, but I don't even try to hide them from students. Sixth-grade teachers offer to take my last class, so I can go home. Their kindness brings fresh tears; I seem to have no control over them.

Once I arrive at home, the couch welcomes me. Larry is in Memphis for a video shoot, so I eat an apple for supper. My body feels flattened by a truck.

I thought I understand feelings of depression; PMS, post-partum blues and depression after major surgery gave me a taste. But this feeling? I'm hollow. Nothing interests me. I don't care about anything and am physically wiped out. I can't go to school tomorrow. I keep thinking, "I can't go on like this. I can't work; I need help."

Tuesday, November 19

As soon as I wake up I call my doctor for an appointment <u>today</u>. I see my doctor's associate, and she prescribes Wellbutrin once a day. My mental state must be obvious; she asks me if I have suicidal thoughts, but I don't. I just don't care. She makes me an appointment for two weeks.

Despite exhaustion all day, I grade a few papers and try to work on a paper for Trevecca, but I spend most of the day on the couch, sleeping or drifting.

I remember feeling this exhaustion after Mama's death, not realizing that I was depressed that whole school year. The depression was not this severe, but I felt tired all the time. My first priority now is to conserve energy; I must work on papers for the next Trevecca class meeting.

Saturday, Nov. 23

Finished teaching the rest of the week and made it to the swimming pool on Friday. I'm a little shaky in the morning, but I can't tell if the medicine is working. Thursday depression hit me again after school, but when the power went off at home, the distraction helped.

Thank you, God, for days I'm not in the pit.

This I Know Now:

I wish I had learned to let go of the "Why?" question sooner. Greenspan's statement makes so much sense now, "Mysteries of death cannot be understood by a rational analytic mind."[44]

I don't regret beginning antidepressants in 2003; I know I felt dead inside and had no resources to continue functioning. I seldom took the time to reread my journals, or I would have seen the slow build up to profound depression.

Now I Am Thankful for:

- the support of teachers in my building during a critical day of grief
- the quick appointment at my doctor's office and a responsive doctor
- the beautiful letter from Jennifer's co-counselor giving me another insight into Jennifer's influence and faith.

Your Turn:

- Don't worry about ANYTHING
- Pray about EVERYTHING, especially

  _____

- Tell God what I need
- Thank Him for all He has done.

Philippians 4:6-7

> *Then you will experience God's peace, which exceeds anything we can understand. His peace will guard your hearts and minds as you live in Christ Jesus. NLT*

A LETTER FROM LIZ

(arrived with the scrapbooks)

I met Jennifer and Danielle the day that we were assigned to our TP (teepee instead of a cabin). I was a little apprehensive of being with two people I didn't know, but from the very beginning, we knew God had placed us together. There was such a bond there that I had never experienced in my previous sessions at camp. Right after we met, we sat down and began to share our testimonies and prayed together; it was as if we had known each other so much longer than just a few minutes. It was a God-sent unity and those four terms were incredible, not because we had wonderful campers but because we had each other. When you work so closely with someone as we did you get to see their heart and who they really are when they are tired and worn out.

Our campers would gather around Jennifer's bed to hear "Josh stories"; she told us how they met and started dating and they were waiting to kiss. It was so incredible to hear her strength and her integrity in the way she lived her life. She brought so much honesty to devotionals, and she loved our girls so much. She never put on a face – she was always real in the way she approached life. I was challenged and blessed by her honesty and the way she lived.

Sunday night I was in church singing and I just kept on thinking that she was in God's presence singing those songs to Him and how amazing that must be for her. She was so faithful in her life; I can't understand why, but God must have said to her "well done my good and faithful servant. You have been so faithful with the life that I have given you, and you have accomplished what I sent you to do …Come and share in my happiness …Come Home."

Chapter 11
WANDERINGS

God's creation is a marvelous gift,
and I count it as joy!

November 2002

Thanksgiving

Holidays are a bridge over the river of memories. I peer over the railing and glimpse objects that trigger a response: a ring for the Christmas she became engaged, an apple for Grandmother's Dutch apple pie every Thanksgiving, a Strawberry Shortcake nightgown for a Halloween costume, black patent shoes (size 2) for Easter Sunday. Anticipating memories of last year's Thanksgiving fill me with dread, so we follow the advice in Charlie Walton's book - "get out of town."

Weeks before Thanksgiving we make reservations for a Southwest flight to Kansas City. Larry's brother, Gary, met us at the airport to drive the hour west to Topeka. Ruthann had a hot supper and warm hugs waiting for us. My heart filled with joy to also see Bethann, their daughter, along with her family; they live in Texas and we don't often see them. When Gary and Ruthann brought Bethann home from the hospital, I spent several days diaper-changing, bottle-warming, and baby-holding that sweet little infant.

Each day of the weekend eased into its own rhythm of cooking, eating, and shopping. I squeezed in some time to grade essays and work on my dissertation. Approval finally arrived for my proposal, and time is short for implementation.

Many years ago, we lived in Topeka and attended the same church as Gary and Ruthann, so Sunday arrived with some unknowns. Attending Sunday School did not revive any old memories for me, but anticipating going to worship slowly pushed a familiar fullness into my chest. I did not trust these feelings, so Larry and I left early.

The trip to Kansas distracted us, just as planned, especially meeting Bethann's red-headed two-year-old Riley. We said our goodbyes at the house before heading back to Kansas City Monday morning. A few tears fell when I hugged Bethann and Ruthann.

We didn't hear from Josh over the holidays. Last Thanksgiving Josh and Jennifer joined my family at a cabin in a state park for dinner, and then they drove down to his family's home.

I carefully keep those memories in a safe place, out of sight.

Cold November days remind me of weekend visits with Josh and Jennifer. I kept ingredients on hand for making home-made soup and cornbread for their unexpected visits.

December 15

Best Friend's Wedding

Courtney and Jennifer were roommates their junior year at Tennessee Tech while Robert and Josh lived with a houseful of engineering students at Tech. Jennifer was expected to be maid of honor at Courtney and Robert's wedding; Josh served as a groomsman. Larry and I both attended the wedding rehearsal since Larry planned to videotape the wedding and I had a part to play at the wedding. Managing the logistics of lighting and camera placement kept Larry busy, as I waited in the lobby with the groomsmen. Watching the guys clowning, fake wrestling, being silly made me wish for Jennifer's presence.

Josh escorted me in before the wedding, and then ushered me out, instead of walking with a bridesmaid. I served as Jennifer's stand-in. The program listed Jennifer as maid of honor along with a short tribute to her. The hole in my heart ached during and after this second wedding she missed.

Sunday, I just can't make it to church. The emotional energy expended Friday and Saturday leaves me depleted, vegetating on the couch all morning. Such low energy all during the day. Sentimental Christmas songs or stories prompt tears; I cry out to God to relieve this pain and comfort me.

A Phone Call from Kansas

The phone rings, and a woman quietly begins, "A friend told me about your loss. Can you talk a few minutes?"

I know immediately who she is. Her daughter was killed by a drunk driver about the same time our Jennifer died. Before we left Kansas in November, Larry's brother told me the story of this family's tragic loss. Gary thought I could help the mother.

Helping others has been part of my DNA since high school while teaching children with special needs provided years of experience responding to pleas for help.

When I hear her voice, I first think, "Maybe I can do this." I typically say "Yes" first, and then have second thoughts.

As we talk, compare traumas, share feelings, panic builds like a balloon buried inside my chest, swelling deep within my soul. The longer we talk, the more it swells. Overwhelmed, I think, "I'm drowning."

I interrupt her and say, "I can't do this anymore. I'm, I'm sorry." I hang up.

Foolishly, I forget that these complicated feelings lie quietly in my heart, surprising me when they show up at unsuspecting moments. The physical pain from these feelings is almost as strong as the emotional stress.

My head knows that my experiences of coping with loss and grief might be helpful to others who walk the same valley. But my pain is too fresh; I can barely cope. My heart knows I cannot share these experiences without being pulled into the pit of mourning.

Christmas Break, 2002

The last week of school before Christmas keeps my mind off the next land-mine, but Friday afternoon driving home from school heartache consumes me. Anticipation of Christmas at our house just isn't there. I can't bear to pull out decorations. But my heart treasures a seed of hope for our family gathering this year.

Last December (2001) my brothers and I planned a Christmas family re-union in Gulf Shores with as many children and spouses as possible. We re-served a large house on the beach for December 2002; as Christmas nears this year, I am so glad to have a plan for getting out of town. Jennifer loved the beach, as I do; our family camped on the Gulf Coast during Spring Break, and Jennifer went several times with friends or on church retreats.

The Sunday morning before Christmas day, I catch a ride with David and Brenda to Paul's house in Montgomery. After a quick stop at Paul's, we drive down to Gulf Shores. Paul's family will arrive tomorrow. Our rental house is past Gulf Shores at Fort Morgan; without highway signs announcing each small town on the Alabama Gulf Coast, it all blends together. Since we are the first to arrive, we inspect the house and claim bedrooms. A big open floor plan furnishes space for cooking, eating, and lounging with a view of the beach; bedrooms fill the second and third floors. I choose a small bedroom on the second floor decorated in soft pastel beach colors. One window faces the beach and opens to a small porch. I immediately push up windows, step out on the porch, and take a deep breath, inhaling the sea air. Blue skies and 70° welcome me to one of my favorite places. The first whiff of salt air opens my soul while worries roll off my shoulders like waves. My fragile soul finds healing.

After eating a simple supper, I fall asleep to the lazy rhythm of waves.

Monday, Dec. 23

Clouds and wind waken me this morning, and it's too windy to sit on my porch for morning meditation. We grab jackets for a walk on the beach as we wait for the rest of the family to arrive. Steve and Marie are joined by their children Andrew and Sara, along with her husband, Matt. Paul's family arrives.

During lunch we catch up on news, sometimes everyone talking at once and then we plan meals. Everyone pitches in cooking and cleaning up; we've done this enough to know each other's preferences.

Daily afternoon walks become the norm as we scour the beach for shells. By evening the wind has strengthened and the waves build, but our loud card games drown out the weather. During the night wind whipping outside my windows wakes me from a deep sleep. By 2:00 A.M. I find Steve and David watching the TV reports of tornado watches. Huge waves break as the wind builds, but eventually, the danger passes, and we wander back to bed.

Tuesday, Dec. 24

Clouds remain this morning, but the sky changes almost every hour. When it darkens, an oil derrick out in the Gulf disappears; then suddenly the sky clears, and a brilliant sun welcomes us to enjoy God's creation. Temperatures warm to 70° again, so we divide into small groups for more walks on the beach. We discover giant cockle shells deposited on the beach after the storm: black, striped, and often damaged, but each shell is worthy of consideration. We learn to take plastic bags with us on our walks for our treasures.

Being with family is easy, especially now, for they are mindful of my fragile state. This family of three brothers and three sisters-in-law understands each other enough to know not to pry or push plans or conversation. Every day I relax a little more.

This afternoon when a group gathers in front of the TV to watch a video, Marie asks me if I know what this movie is about. I thought I did, but she says a young woman dies in it. I change my plans and make a nest in my tranquil turquoise room to read. I am so thankful she warned me.

Wednesday, Dec. 25

This morning when I awaken I can't hear a whisper of waves through my open windows. Layers of thick blue and gray clouds constantly change the sky over a calm sea. Much of the day is spent preparing a traditional turkey and ham dinner for our Christmas celebration. Several years ago, we gave up giving each other presents; once children married and then grandchildren were born the logistics were too complicated.

In the afternoon we drive over to Fort Morgan State Historic Site to roam the grounds of an old Civil War fort. Brick archways, floors, and walls bear the effects of years of harsh weather. Despite the chilly wind this bunch of nerds is fascinated by the fort.

A spectacular sunset has us grabbing cameras to capture God's paintbrush at work. With the glassy sea as a mirror, tonight's setting sun reflects coral pink on a soft blue, still ocean.

Thursday, Dec. 26.

Paul and his family leave for north Alabama, meeting at Tricia's parents' house for another celebration. Sara and Matt travel to Arkansas to do the same with Matt's family. The rest of us take long naps and long walks on the beach before heading into town to see *Lord of the Rings 2*.

Friday, Dec. 27

The crowd is down to six today, so Brenda, Marie and I drive to the outlet mall in Foley, Alabama for some after-Christmas bargains. We meet Steve, David, and Andrew for dinner at a restaurant for some fresh fish. Suddenly, as I sit in the midst of family, a question pops into my head, "How can my vibrant daughter be gone?" Tears threaten, and I swallow the lump in my throat. If anyone at the table notices, they don't say anything. The potential for a crisis passes. Having others ignore my distress, rather than hovering, inquiring, "Are you okay?" works best for me.

Sunday, Dec. 29

Arrived home Saturday and woke up this morning with a stomach virus. I soon realize that the trip to the beach distracted me from my worst sad moments. I wonder how Christmas has been for Josh. The memory of just one year ago must have been on his mind. Christmas night Josh and Jennifer were at hour house. That night he gave Jennifer her engagement ring.

Wednesday, Jan. 1, 2003

I weep all day, lying on the couch watching HGTV. Even when we eat out at a restaurant I cannot stop my tears. Larry's greatest gift to me now is that he never complains when this despair comes. He just lets me "be," and that seems to be what I need.

Thursday, Jan. 2, 2003

Morning brings new energy, grading papers, cleaning house, cooking, shopping, talking with friends on the phone.

Where does this energy come from? Thank you, God, for days like this.

Josh called last night full of stories of fly fishing and getting stuck in the mud. He's returning to Virginia.

> *Lord, bless Josh in his travels and outings. Give him just*
> *what he needs to learn to live without Jennifer.*

This month Larry resigned from his work at our church as a video director; he now works full time at home with his free-lance video business, Souder Productions. At the same time, we also change our church home and return to Woodmont Hills, the church we attended when we moved to Nashville in 1978.

The change in church home does two things for us: people and memories at Madison can be avoided, and at Woodmont, we can be anonymous. We do not know many of the newer members there, can sit near the back, and leave quickly. But it is also a familiar place; through our moves out of town and to different parts of Nashville, it continues to feel like home. Church continues to hold landmines of memories and heart-breaking despondency.

Friday, Jan. 3, 2003

Reading in *Utmost* today I find the reference in Hebrews 11:8 where Abraham obeys God, not knowing where he was going. Chambers challenges me, asking if I've been questioning God, asking Him, "What are You going to do?" Chambers asserts that God does not tell me what He will do; He reveals who He is to me. God speaks to me; not by visions and dreams, but by words.[45]

This major change in our lives – a different place to worship, feels like a space has opened as we wait for God to reveal Himself to us. We have new options for service, but maybe we need to be fed first.

The trip to the beach is a treasured memory because it felt like days of healing. My pictures reveal the beautiful sunrises and sunsets on a winter beach. Just looking at one of those pictures leads me back to that peaceful time.

God's creation is a marvelous gift, and I count it as joy!

This I Know Now:

Even today the memories and comfort of that Christmas trip to the beach can give me peace. I felt surrounded and supported by my family, and God's creation soothed my troubled soul. Some Christmases have been easier than others, Larry's best gifts to me are trips to the beach, no matter what time of the year.

I've learned about creating emotional boundaries through the years but recently have found help in thinking about them beforehand. I have a nurse practitioner who talks me through situations that hold landmines; making a plan provides me with options to avoid the explosions.

Now I Am Thankful for:

- the distractions with Larry's family in Topeka for Thanksgiving.
- having a different place to worship but still having friends there
- learning my limits through painful emotions

Your Turn:

- Don't worry about ANYTHING
- Pray about EVERYTHING
- Tell God what I NEED, not what I want

- THANK Him for all He has done.

Philippians 4:6-7

> *Then you will experience God's peace, which exceeds anything we can understand. His peace will guard your hearts and minds as you live in Christ Jesus. NLT*

Chapter 12
VALLEY-DEEP

When you finally get to the mountaintop,
give thanks for the valley you've just been through.
Because you will almost certainly go there again.
And again, it will be hard, but it will be good.
—Jan Karon[46]

I often refer to my times of grieving as walking through the valley of the shadow of death as David wrote in Psalm 23. In these last few months, I've stumbled around, sometimes losing my way. I could feel the Shepherd with me but didn't seek His comfort. On the darkest days, I am like a sheep that doesn't have a clue where the path is. The valley is surrounded by mountains and woods with no path or river to guide me. Some days I can't find my way out.

New Beginnings, 2003

Saturday was the first class of the new semester at Trevecca; seeing cohort friends at the beginning of a new course always energizes me.

Sunday's sermon topic addressed Job's question, "Why me, Lord?" During songs I keep my guard up; tears are so close to the surface, and I can't face those huge emotions. After church I realize the strain of holding myself together. After this emotional tension, I am as flat as the glassy Gulf at Christmas. Will this be another day on the couch? Thankfully, after a nap, I'm able to work on my dissertation.

Our first day back to work after Christmas break, January 6, is a day without students, giving us all time to get organized again. Blessings for us all.

January 18

Seven inches of snow on the ground and a temperature below 0° welcomes us this morning. How thankful I am for a warm place, plenty of food in the pantry and frig, and best of all, no school.

Cooking soup on winter days remind me again of those wonderful times Jennifer and Josh came home and ate with us. She shared stories of cooking adventures in nutrition class or making homemade pasta. I treasure those memories. Haven't heard from Josh in two weeks; I'll call him today.

Larry went to her room last night and remarked how sad it is to see Jennifer's clothes in the closet, just some jackets and a coat. Maybe in the spring we can rearrange her room and close some doors to painful memories.

January 19

Continuing Despair

Sometimes I have so little motivation and seem to be just going through the motions of living. On this long snowy weekend, I am content to stay at home. Larry goes to a party for a friend from the Woodmont church without me, because I can't face so many who would hug me and love me. Sometimes I've gone to events without thinking through the consequences, so now I try to anticipate before committing. Larry returns with greetings from many friends

When will the pain ease? I am careful not to listen to any songs with memories or look at pictures of Jennifer. Her room waits for cleaning and sorting, but I cannot face it.

A darkness entered our lives on April 13, 2002, and infinite sadness waits in the shadows to drown me with tears. I guard my heart carefully because these feelings completely drain me.

I continue to look for a clearer understanding of this grief. This passage from Chambers seems to be written just for me:

The time to listen is when a darkness comes. When God gives a vision, and darkness follows - WAIT. Never try to help God fulfill His word.

Consider Abram. God promised him a son and then was silent for 13 years. Abram no longer could rely on himself; his self-sufficiency was destroyed. Those years were a time of discipline - not God's displeasure.[47]

Sunday, January 27

Seeing old friends at Woodmont does not set off my tears. Meaningful worship lifts my heart to heaven while other songs trigger complex emotions from the first note.

Sunday, February 2

We go to the early service and see many old friends. Rubel's sermon this morning is on the sacrifice of Isaac. The story of Abraham placing his son on an altar of wood becomes personal with this lesson. We gave up our only child, but it was not our choice. I don't think I could have done what Abraham did to show God he trusted Him.

Saturday, February 8

Josh calls this week. It's beginning to look like he won't be able to take off this summer for travel to Colorado and Canada. He doesn't know what to do with his life right now. Search for a job? Complete his thesis? He thinks of all the plans he made with Jennifer and seems to have lost his direction. Research and classwork overwhelm him.

I can relate to the pressure of deadlines. I don't know how to advise him, but maybe he just needs a listening ear.

Courtney calls, and she's having trouble sleeping. Her grief seems to be even more intense now than those early days and weeks.

Lord, help our breaking hearts.

Sunday, February 16

Coming home Thursday, memories of Jennifer and Josh last year at Valentine's Day flood my heart. She traveled to Virginia Tech to be with Josh. They made homemade pasta and created an elegant meal. So much fun.

After functioning well at school on Friday, I walk in the valley that night. Am I headed toward another bottomless depression? Rain for 48 hours doesn't help my mood. When I feel this grief, I know I need to avoid even looking at pictures of Jennifer.

Should I see a counselor? It's time to go back to the doctor and get a refill on Wellbutrin. Almost a year since her death and I still have random times when I think she can't be dead.

Where are you, God?
Why didn't you save my Jennifer?"
What is the point of her death?"
How long does this deep pain and despair last?

March 5

Posthumous Award for Jennifer

Two months before her death, Jennifer applied for a 2002-2003 scholarship through the Nashville Family and Consumer Sciences Association. She earned the scholarship but did not live to receive it.

The Consumer Science Dept. at Tennessee Tech invite Larry and me to attend an awards ceremony in March. Since Larry is in Chicago working, I ask my close friend, Emalie to join me. We drive to Cookeville after school, eat some dinner, and locate the consumer science building on campus. In lieu of the scholarship Jennifer earned, the association donated money and cookbooks to the School of Human Ecology in her memory.

Excerpt from the presentation by Jennifer's advisor:

Briefly, but profoundly, Jennifer Souder passed through
our lives as an active, involved student at Tennessee Tech.

We remember her as studying Human Ecology ...but her MAJOR was life ...pouring her life, that is the life she lived in Christ, into those around her. I believe she would say through HIM, that is Christ, she excelled.

Academically, Jennifer was a Dean's List student and a teacher's dream student ...desiring knowledge and the improvement of skills. She served as captain of the Spring Team at TTU and a member of the Fellowship of Christian Athletes where she met her fiancé, Josh Sesler. She went beyond in the field of athletics competing as a triathlete and instilling in youth her love for sports in summer camps.

These beautiful words are music to a mother's heart; I learn again how Jennifer's life blessed those around her. She had no idea that God's glory just poured out of her.

It is a touching program, but I found it so difficult to keep my emotions under control. Tears flowed.

Saturday, March 15

Assignments for Trevecca consume much of my time. An abscessed tooth last weekend and a root canal on Tuesday find me in physical pain.

Josh came two weeks ago with a big bushy beard for a brief visit on Saturday He hopes to finish coursework this semester, work the month of June, and travel in July. He seems okay, but it's hard to know on short visits.

The pain of grief is not better. I am about thirty seconds from tears at any time, expecting a suffocating wave of emotion to hit. Rex, a friend from Miami, called. He and Brenda had a child die while they were missionaries in Papua New Guinea. He says, "When people say you'll get over this, they are wrong."

Courtney came by the school on Wednesday to visit while I ate lunch. She and Robert are now living in Texas, and she seems to be in a good place. We talked about the first year of marriage, finding a place of worship, and catching up on news of mutual friends

The closer it gets to April, the sadder I am. The one-year anniversary. I don't want to even think about it. The woman from Kansas calls again and talks to Larry; I don't want to talk to her. I can't. The emotional drain of talking about grief empties the spaces in my soul; I'm learning I must take care of me first.

March 30

One Year Anniversary

"Holiness or Hardness Toward God?" today's reading today in *My Utmost for His Highest*. Chambers says that "many of us stop praying and become hard toward God because we have only an emotional interest in prayer. When we lose sight of God, we become hard and dogmatic. Our prayers are more lists of demands, things we need (or want?), rather than reaching up for that holy relationship with God."[48]

I don't think I've become hard, but I have stopped praying.

The business of writing a dissertation, plus the regular load of school work, crowd out my quiet times with God. My work excludes God. Even though I am aware of needing those quiet moments, I don't seem to find a way to make them a priority. Random moments at church can release a flood of tears.

Last night we ate dinner at Safari's restaurant. When we were seated, memories engulf me. This is the same booth where we sat with Josh and Jennifer last year, her last visit home. A week later she was dead. I tell Larry, "This is where we sat a year ago with Josh and Jennifer." He immediately asks if I want to move and then signals the waitress for a table change. Neither of us realized it was our first time to eat at the restaurant since her death. Landmines are everywhere!

The closer the days come to April 13, the more flashes of moments of those days invade my heart. I'm not sure what to do on that day. Using Langston Hughes' poem, "What Happens to a Dream Deferred?", I wrote this poem to express my feelings.

April
by Joy Martell Souder

What happens to a grief deferred?
Does it bubble up inside when memories wash over me?
Or is it like a hard scab to be forgotten
until the wound is exposed and screams with pain?
When does the pain ease?
Will spring always bring fresh memories
of the days we buried her?
Is it easier to defer this grief?
or does it make it worse?
Some days I feel held together with fine cotton thread
that could break at any moment.

April 12-13

Leaning Together

A busy weekend keeps the rawest of pain away. I mentally hold memories of Jennifer away, so I won't feel the pain. This quote from Wangerin's helps me —"When the heart is ready, the mind will allow the knowledge down."[49] He is referring to the stage of shock when the griever just can't believe the death occurred. But I also believe that when my heart is ready, my mind will allow memory and feelings to invade my heart.

Saturday afternoon Josh comes over for a short visit, and we make plans to meet at church on Sunday. Later in the day I drive to Dickson, TN to meet David and Steve and their wives for dinner. Even a short visit with family helps me cope. We tell stories from childhood, a great visit.

Josh and Greg meet Larry and me at Woodmont Church Sunday morning and afterward Lauren, Greg's sister and one of Jennifer's friends, joins us for lunch. A visit with Josh and friends always makes me feel closer to Jennifer. I tell them a story about Jennifer when she was in the second grade. Josh has not heard this one. While her second-grade class stood in line outside, Jennifer suddenly turned a cartwheel. Her teacher sent her to the office – the only time in her school life; she was completely devastated! But it made Josh proud to hear of her energy and impulsiveness!

Sunday afternoon Lark, Belinda, and Kathy from the girlfriends' group at Woodmont come over with their husbands to plant a saucer magnolia bush in the backyard in Jennifer's memory. Josh joins us as we dig the hole, pray, and remember her life. It is a good way to spend April 13. Josh's mom calls me later in the day.

I take personal leave days on Monday and Tuesday to participate in a memorial run/walk/bike at Tennessee Tech. Last year Larry and I participated when so many high schoolers and college students wanted a way to remember Jennifer's dedication to being healthy and active. Since Larry must be out-of-town, I drive to Cookeville Monday and stay with the preacher and his family. About fifty people participate this year, and it helps me to see teens and college friends who loved Jennifer. The Tech students from Jennifer's class graduate this spring.

The beauty of this season reminds me of last spring. I sift and select memories I want to savor but try to limit these times of remembering. Memories are like a wound covered with a bandage; I don't want to rip the band-aid off because it will hurt too much.

April 20

Taking Stock

So where am I in this journey? I continue to take Wellbutrin for depression and have not hit the horrible low that occurred in November. A week ago, Sunday night my defenses were shattered with contractions of physical pain but by mid-day Monday I felt better.

It amazes me how the despair appears without warning and may not be related to anything I'm reading, watching, thinking, or doing. It truly is physical. What makes this happen?

Guarding my heart continues to be my focus for well-being. Her room still waits. The extra furniture from her Cookeville apartment is crammed into her room with only a path cleared for walking through.

I want to work on her pictures and displays for her room, but my heart must be protected. I haven't listened to my CDs of Christian music in a month since my CD player was stolen out of my car. I carefully edit the songs I can listen to, so I don't burst into tears.

May 17

Another Wedding, More Memories

A long month with no journaling or quiet time. It has been too hard – I just don't want to think or remember.

We place membership at Woodmont, and Larry signs up to be a reader or lead prayer in worship. I have no desire to get involved in a ministry. Most Sundays I can sit through a service without weeping, progress!

The last marriage of the group of engineering guys who roomed together at Tech took place this weekend. Brad and Becky connect to Josh and Jennifer in layers; Becky and Jennifer rode mountain bikes in the summers, Becky is Robert's sister, and Brad's dad and I are friends from our work at Trevecca.

During the reception I watch all these friends reunite and enjoy being together. Deep fissures of pain shatter my defenses as I mourn the loss of Jennifer and Josh's wedding day. As quickly as possible I say my good-byes and drive home. Suffocating physical pain steals my breath, but I cannot stop the tears. Emotional exhaustion puts me on the couch all day Sunday, and Monday I am still emotional.

May 24

Another Award Ceremony

Last May my assistant principal suggested that we give an award to an eighth-grader in Jennifer's memory. I gave it some thought, discussed it with the eighth-grade teachers, and developed some guidelines. We named it the "Jennifer Souder Humanitarian Award." A large trophy is given to the honoree, while a plaque in the office includes names selected each year. This first year of the award I choose Monica because of her heart of service. She demonstrates in many ways the same willingness to help others as Jennifer did.

At our end-of-the-year awards ceremony, Emalie makes the presentation for me. I watch from the second level of the gym. Afterward, I weep through the hugs and leave the classroom to regain control.

How hard it was! This protective shell around my heart is my only way to cope with the pain. It is exhausting to work so hard to stay under control.

May 25 is the day Josh and Jennifer had planned to be married. I'm thankful to be in Kentucky, visiting both of Mama's sisters, their daughters, and a granddaughter.

Email from Brother, David

> *Isn't it nice to be surprised by an unexpected blooming flower? See, flowers can bloom for you again. And the sun can shine for you, too. It's just been a very, very long winter for you. Eventually, your metamorphized self will emerge from its cocoon, in its own time. You will be changed, but you will be ok.*

This I Know Now:

In my recent discovery of the Enneagram (a method of typing personality) I've learned that my <u>motivation</u> is to be self-reliant and stay in control of my situation. My <u>fear</u> is to not have that control. Now I see that those times when I felt my emotions threatening to drown me or suffocate me were about control. I knew I would not be able to control my sobbing – not just leaking tears or crying, but loud blubbering, mouth covered, arms wrapped around my waist. My usual response in those moments was to escape as noted in this chapter. The emotional and physical price usually happened almost immediately, as if a rush of adrenalin had left me depleted.

Now I Am Thankful for:

- memories of the ceremonies that honored Jennifer's life
- learning to listen to God through those dark days
- knowing that He never left me even when I did not seek Him.

Your Turn:

- Don't worry about ANYTHING
- Pray about EVERYTHING
- Tell God what I NEED
- THANK Him for all He has done.
- In my circumstance today, I may not be able to see His gifts and blessings, but I can find at least three blessings today.

  _____

  _____

  _____

Philippians 4:6-7

> *Then you will experience God's peace, which exceeds anything we can understand. His peace will guard your hearts and minds as you live in Christ Jesus. NLT*

Chapter 13
PIECES

*I protect myself from the pain of grief
by not going to events or places
where I will be reminded of Jennifer.*

Summer, 2003

In June, I slowly begin to emerge from my darkest days, but the same unpredictable pattern of my first year of grief occurs: spurts of improvement and then long treks into pain and sadness in the valley of grief.

June 30

A beautiful sunny and cool Saturday morning: clear blue skies, a soft breeze gently moves through the backyard tulip poplar tree.

I've been unable to write in a journal for a month. I can't pray or study my Bible. I just can't take the chance of crying or feeling emotional.

I protect myself from pain by not going to events or places where I will be touched or reminded of Jennifer. I choose not to go to weddings or funerals – too many landmines. At home, I feel safe. If a memory threatens to push me into despair at home, I can go to another room to distract myself.

In the past two weeks, I find myself finally able to tackle some projects upstairs. First, I decide on a complete makeover of my office, fresh paint, a wallpaper border, new table skirt, curtains, and re-arrangement of furniture. Once this room is complete I am ready to move on to her bedroom. Jennifer's room is jammed with furniture and a mishmash of her belongings.

Sorting through the pieces of Jennifer's life, my heart is downcast, but I'm not heading into a major depression. Then a migraine slowly emerges; it lasts for two days. Despite the pain I keep plugging away at sorting through all her belongings at my own pace.

I think she saved every piece of paper - from Hello Kitty notebooks to journals crammed with her habitual lists of items to pack for camp. By the end of the week I see real progress, and the migraine is gone. Most of her clothes and college memorabilia were given away a year ago, so all that is left are the keepsakes from preschool to high school.

One day Larry asks me, "How can you work in her room? For a whole year you could not stand to even go in her room."

"I don't know," I answer. "It just feels like I can move ahead with this. Summer planning prepared my 'head' to sort, clean, and organize; her room is just the next project on my list."

Working through these memories gives me time to process and contemplate some "what ifs." What if she had lived? Jennifer and Josh's May wedding would be over now, and my sorting and organizing would be the next logical step. Either way, this room's purpose shifts from Jennifer's room to a multi-functional room - my sewing and crafts as well as a guest room.

Finally, I frame her school pictures and arrange them in the upstairs hall chronologically. Once completed, every time I walk up the stairs, I see her little four-year-old preschool face, every grade school picture, the awkward middle school days, and high school senior pictures. Somehow these pictures comfort me, keeping those years in my heart. I know the longer they remain on the wall they will eventually become like wallpaper, not a conscious memory, but for now, those pictures tell her life story.

Change in Relationship with God

In between the summer projects, every minute is consumed with writing my dissertation; I use busy-ness as an excuse for not seeking God.

The nagging question, "why?" continues to eat away my inner self. I've lost a tangible connection with the Father, and my anchor rests on shifting ground. The following quote from Wolterstorff captures my state of mind:

> I cannot fit it all together by saying, '" God decided it was time for her to come home" but neither can I say, "There was nothing He could do about it." I cannot fit it all together. I can only, with Job, endure. I do not know why God did not prevent Jennifer's (my substitution) death. To live without the answer is precarious. It's hard to keep one's footing.[50]

During the school year my habit of prayer, Scripture study, and journaling completely disappeared, and I did not renew it when summer arrived. Working on her bedroom provided some progress in healing, but I neglect the important "soul-work." A friend compares this soul-work to carrying around a suitcase full of the baggage of our lives. It needs emptying every morning, so I can begin the day fresh with an empty suitcase. If I skip a morning of soul-work, the suitcase overflows.

Gradually, I realize a slow anger simmers within me.

Journal Entry

> Josh finally called last night. Hadn't heard from him in a month. He sounded great; he didn't have phone service in Montana. He spent two weeks with his dad camping, hiking, and rafting. Now he is in Durango, Colorado at Kamp Kanakuk, the last camp Jennifer and Josh worked together. The camp staff dedicated the chapel to Jennifer; Josh likes to study in there. He says he's been facing some memories – things he had forgotten.

July

My second summer session of residence on Trevecca's campus arrives in early July. Our cohort group plows through Chapter 2 of our dissertations, reviewing all the literature pertaining to our research. We also attend nine hours of classes, write papers, and make presentations. Since this is the second time to experience these hectic days, I know I must budget my time to meet all the deadlines. Chapter 2 of the dissertation is due at the end of the summer.

Near the end of our seven-day term, I wake up one morning extremely ill; I struggle to dress and go to class but end up needing help to return to my dorm. I'm vomiting so much I must stay in bed; maybe it's food poisoning, but we all ate the same thing last night. I finally call Larry and ask him to bring me first aid: crackers, Gatorade, and Pepto Bismol. Once I keep down several doses of Pepto and lay very, very still, my stomach remains calm. The workload for this program does not provide time off for sickness, and as soon as I am able, I return to classes and complete the term.

I see an internist as soon as I return home. He does an ultrasound on my gallbladder and discovers a pyramid of gallstones. I send an email to my cohort group telling them I am stoned in Nashville! Before school begins in the fall, I have gallbladder surgery of the easiest kind – no cutting. These less invasive surgeries certainly speed up recovery time, but as in-service begins, I find my energy quickly dissipates.

School Year Begins

When we return to school, I enlist help with the physical work in my classroom; however, I worry about having the energy to stay on my feet once school begins. Those first few days with students are critical for establishing rapport and connection with students. Setting routines and learning names are a priority for me, and I want to be "on top of my game."

The days in August and September require every ounce of my energy to get through each class period. Slowly, slowly my energy returns, but I am still drowning in the valley of grief and pain over Jennifer's death.

The progress I made in the summer slipped away when I had the gallbladder attack and then surgery. Now I'm struggling with deadlines for this last year at Trevecca. Research has to be completed, the final two chapters of the dissertation written and approved, along with two more courses: fall and spring semesters, and then one more summer session.

Two steps forward, then three steps back.

I Sent You a Helicopter

We sent you two boats and a helicopter!
What were you expecting?

You've heard the story about the man stranded on his rooftop during a great flood. A boat comes by, and the rescue worker says, "Get in!" The man waves him on saying, "I trust God to save me."

The water gets higher, and another boat comes. The man on the roof yells, "Go on. I'm waiting for God to send a miracle." Finally, his head is barely above water as he clutches the limb of a tree while a helicopter hovers over him. When a ladder is lowered, he does not reach for it because he is sure God will save him. Of course, he drowns. When he arrives at the gates of heaven, he sees Peter and asks, "Why didn't God save me? I trusted in Him!"

Peter shakes his head and answers, "We sent you two boats and a helicopter! What were you expecting?"

October 2003

In the first few weeks of school, our band director receives a transfer to become an assistant principal at another middle school. We are happy for him, and it gives Keith, our chorus teacher, the opportunity to teach band, his first love. But we suddenly need a new chorus teacher.

It just so happens (or God has a hand in this) that we know a great chorus teacher who wants to teach middle school. Last spring Lora, Keith's student teacher, fit well with our eighth-grade team's philosophy. Since the music department classrooms are on the same hall as the eighth grade, our team has daily contact with the band and chorus teachers. We observed Lora up close and personal. Through years of supervising many student teachers, I've learned some candidates for teaching are naturals, and Lora has those instincts. We quickly discovered she "had the goods" to teach middle school: excellent student communication and that innate teacher "radar" to deal with discipline issues.

Most student teachers quickly learn they either love middle school or hate it; finding someone who loves middle school who also is a natural at teaching is rare. Lora is presently working in an elementary school but is eager to return to middle school. After a few administrative phone calls to obtain the necessary approvals for a transfer, she happily makes the change to our school mid-semester and settles in across the hall from me.

The eighth-grade team helps Lora move in and set up her classroom. Her schedule includes general music classes, chorus, and one seventh-grade reading class. With an abundance of reading materials, I share books and ideas while we brainstorm plans for her reading class. She is thrilled to be teaching middle school chorus and confident she can meet the challenge of a reading class.

Has God sent me a boat? This young woman bubbles with energy and enthusiasm, and she just happens to work across the hall from me. I can't help but notice that Lora and Jennifer were born the same year.

As Lora and I get to know each other, I carefully keep my heart shielded from strong emotional connections. I cannot afford to give this heart away or extend it to someone. It takes constant emotional and mental control to keep the wall up. A year of grief taught me to guard my broken, shattered heart, so I built a thick wall around it. It is far from mended.

Lora and I have many conversations before and after school, as well as quick moments during the day, sharing funny incidents or problems. Each day we learn bits and pieces of each other's life. We find many things in common; she graduated from Trevecca, and I am still a student there. We both grew up in conservative but different churches.

Since she is looking for a change in her church home, I suggest that she visit our church, Woodmont Hills. After her first visit, she comes to me Monday morning bursting with excitement. "I can't believe I could hear four-part harmony: sopranos, altos, tenors, and basses without instruments!" All her previous worship experiences involved instruments, choirs, soloists and weak participation from the congregation. Our acapella music speaks to the vocalist in her.

After a few more visits to Woodmont, she jumps into church activities. Since we usually attend different services, we seldom see each other at church, but conversations Monday morning fill me in on her experiences. She frequently mentions people she meets whom I have known for years, but she also connects with many people I don't know. She soon tries out to sing with the praise team and is quickly accepted, giving her another circle of people at church I do not know.

Something Is Wrong

Fridays after school often involve a "meeting" at a nearby restaurant, our code word for hanging out together. Most of the eighth-grade teachers show up, but we always invite anyone on staff to join us. Lora becomes a regular at these meetings. Since appetizers are usually the main food course, I don't notice right away that she eats very little on these occasions.

One afternoon after school, as Lora is walking out of her room to go home, we stop to chat as usual. Suddenly she slides down the wall and becomes a puddle on the floor. All day she has been in terrible pain with her wisdom teeth; she has not seen a dentist but needed some relief during the day. I always keep Tylenol and Ibuprofen with me, so I give her some of both at different times during the day. I did not think to ask if she has eaten anything, but by the end of the day, it is clear that she took too much pain medication on an empty stomach. She is in no shape to drive across town to her apartment.

I quickly call Martha, a teammate, who lives close by to see if she can follow us to Lora's apartment. I drive Lora home in her car, and then Martha takes me back to school to get my car. Lora eventually sees a dentist and has oral surgery to pull the offending teeth. My mother-instinct just took over, but no alarm bells went off about Lora having a serious problem.

Bit by bit, Lora opens the door to her secret. This beautiful, slim, young woman controls her weight with self-imposed calorie counts. One afternoon as we stand in my room talking, I question, "There's a problem here with eating, isn't there?"

"How did you know?" She is surprised to learn that I can see her secret. She doesn't realize the many clues she has dropped in our conversations.

And the Connection?

What do I know about eating disorders? Jennifer came home from church camp when she was in middle school with stories about girls her age who were hyper-concerned about their weight. They tried to severely control their portions of food.

In high school Jennifer's best friend suffered from eating disorders. We frequently talked about her concerns about her friend's problem with anorexia. Then one day she came home from school and said, "Mom, I heard A. throwing up in the girls' bathroom today. I know she has a problem with eating." Jennifer observed vigilant parents encourage their daughters to eat and saw how ineffective they were. As a friend she was at a loss to help. She knew close-up the effects of eating disorders, and it influenced her plans for the future.

During Jennifer's last two years in high school, she quit the band and joined the track team as well as cross country. During the off-season, she took kick-boxing classes to keep in shape, as well as maintaining a healthy diet. After three years of pizza and snacks, while performing with the school band, I was happy to see her give more attention to healthy eating.

Following three changes in her major at Tennessee Tech, Jennifer finally settled on Human Ecology in her junior year. In her scholarship application in family and consumer science, she described the path that led her from psychology to nursing to nutrition.

> I came to Tennessee Technological University on a track and field scholarship and planned to major in Psychology. After one year I learned that Psychology was not the field I wanted to pursue. I changed my major to Nursing because I love to reach out and help others. While taking a Nutrition course required for nursing students, I fell in love with learning about food and the way the body handles it. I then changed my major to Human Ecology with an emphasis in Food, Nutrition, and Dietetics. I have enjoyed all the classes I am taking in my new major.
>
> When I graduate with my B.S. degree in May 2003 I hope to further my education by interning under a Dietitian and becoming a Registered Dietitian. I would also like to get my master's degree in Nutrition and Exercise. For

my post-graduate work, I am looking at Virginia Tech University's program. With this extended education, I am considering two options for my career plans. One is to be a practicing dietitian and concentrate on anorexics and bulimics. The second option is to work in sports nutrition, planning and perfecting diet plans for athletes. This would combine my love for sports and nutrition.

Is the Helicopter?

My friendship with Lora grows daily as we face difficult students or challenges in teaching middle school, while at the same time, I learn first-hand the internal conflict a person with an eating disorder constantly battles. Being in control of every calorie consumes her.

My head knows that Lora's presence in my life helps me in many ways. But my heart says, "Thanks, God, but I want my daughter, not a substitute." I don't want to admit this friendship with Lora is a gift from God. When I finally recognize He has sent me exactly the person I need, I resist making an emotional connection, dig in my heels and stubbornly wish for "what was." I still keep my heart guarded. Like so many things God sends my way, I struggle against His plans.

The rescue God planned for me is just beginning.

This I Know Now:

For a year I questioned God, begged, searched for answers, prayed, and studied, but my anger slowly developed as I moved away from Him. Since I did not have a satisfactory answer to the "why" question, I drifted into a new phase of grief, anger at God.

Focusing on another person, in this case, Lora and her needs, is exactly what I needed to pull my head out of my unrelenting grief. I tried to think my way out this trauma, but my gut told me helping Lora would help me.

Now I Am Thankful for:

- that full-circle moment when I realized helping Lora was completing Jennifer's goal of helping those with eating disorders
- working on my dissertation and taking classes at Trevecca engaged my thinking and helped me through some dark times
- the chain of events that led Lora to the classroom across the hall

Your Turn:

- Don't worry about ANYTHING, even

_____

- Pray about EVERYTHING
- Tell God what I need
- Thank Him for all He has done.

Philippians 4:6-7

> *Then you will experience God's peace, which exceeds anything we can understand. His peace will guard your hearts and minds as you live in Christ Jesus. NLT*

Chapter 14
FOOTBRIDGE

*God's purpose is to enable me to see
that He can walk on the storms of my life right now.*
—Oswald Chambers[51]

February 2004

The Girlfriends' Circle

The first sleepover took place in March 1993. A sleepover for six women in their mid-forties. We meet up at the Hilton Suites in Brentwood on a Friday night, eat dinner at a nearby restaurant, return to the hotel for late-night snacks, long talks, and little sleep.

That sleepover gave birth to an annual tradition of a one-night stay at a hotel to eat, laugh, cry, tell stories, and catch up on each other's lives. Each year I document our journey in a journal, writing a summary of our lives for the past year. Before we share our news each year, I read the past year's entry to remind us of the way we were.

We first met each other at the Ashwood church in the 1980s, attending Bible classes together, giving baby showers, volunteering for church workdays. Our children's lives connected in various ways, beginning when some of the children were preschool age or still babies. When In 1990 Larry and I moved north of the Cumberland River to Madison, but still in Nashville, and I missed these good friends. Joan's husband died in January 1993 after a long illness with kidney disease, and we reunited at his funeral to support Joan. A tragedy of one of our own reminded us of the strength of friends. We realized how much we needed each other's support, understanding, and laughter.

Since 1993, our circle has experienced divorce, cancer, death, brain tumor, remarriage, children leaving home, weddings, grandchildren.

In April of 2002, this circle of women surrounded me with their support after Jennifer's death. In March 2003 we had another sleepover. Part of the journal entry:

> This is our tenth spring to meet like this! I felt loved and cared for. Belinda paid for my dinner, and they all covered my part of the hotel bill. Belinda sent me spring flowers on Thursday.
>
> This circle of friends was at my door as soon as they heard the news of Jennifer's death. How comforting they have been. Joan and Belinda came the Saturday night she died, and Kathy, Carrie, and Lark were at my house on Sunday. All year phone calls, cards, gifts in the mail and plans to get together have supported me. We saw the Ya-Ya Sisterhood movie in the summer together.

On the one-year anniversary of Jennifer's death, they brought a tree and planted it in our backyard to remember her life. This saucer magnolia blooms every spring with beautiful pink blossoms that remind me of their steadfast love and my sweet daughter.

In February I contact the circle, asking when we will meet this spring. They all think this is a sign of progress on my part, to reach out and seek their company. After dinner we go see the movie *Calendar Girls,* a story of a group of women who support each other through good and bad. We find it appropriate for us in many ways.

Closing Chapter at Trevecca

On a bright sunny day in May 2004, I slip on a black robe, carefully place the tam (instead of a mortarboard) on my head and adjust the hood for graduation with an Ed.D. at Trevecca. We walk the line, even though we still must complete a summer-in-residence in July as well as complete the dissertation. Graduation creates its own excitement with robes, tams, family from out of town, and Lark, Belinda, and Kathy show up. As soon as final revisions are made on the dissertation, and I make a presentation at the symposium in July, I will officially be called "Dr. Souder."

Despite the delays in approval for my topic, the restrictions placed on my research by my school system, and the stress of deadlines, the experience of earning a doctorate and completing the dissertation in three years gives me great satisfaction. I love the research part of any assignment; incorporating new knowledge and strategies inspires my teaching. This work has been the ultimate distraction during two years of grief. I can walk up the stairs to my office, turn on my computer, and lose my thoughts in writing and research.

On the last day of the summer session in July, we put on our robes again and have a closing ceremony with just our faculty. Three long years of hard work and emotional upheaval! These 24 colleagues, now friends, supported and encouraged me through the most difficult time of my life. A few share their experiences, and as I listen, I know I must share some important things with them. Heart pounding, emotions high, I step up to the front of the room.

> *We've been on a journey together for the past three years, and you have supported and encouraged me in countless ways. On Monday, April 15, 2002, we arrived at our church building for the first visitation for Jennifer's death. Quietly waiting for me were Dr. Welch (Dean of our department) and Dr. Brooks (my advisor). Thank you is not enough to express my gratitude for this program and all your support. Working to reach this goal of graduation engaged my brain to give my heart some space to find its way again.*
>
> *Wolterstorff said, 'Faith is a footbridge that you don't know*

will hold you up over the chasm until you're forced to walk out onto it.' Our first course by Dr. Swink and Dr. Cox showed me the importance of strengthening my own bridge during my darkest days. This cohort held the bridge for me that first summer. Your encouragement, kindness, and support made it possible for me to continue.

In the past year I have realized my spiritual journey has stalled a bit; I've been mad at God, questioning, wondering why He did not save my daughter, why her life, why not mine, why now? The thing is, submerged in my innermost being, I know God has not left me. I left Him, but He has been waiting for me, just off to the side and behind just a bit. Just waiting for me to seek Him, to ask Him to hold me close.

Again, thanks are just not enough.

August

An Invitation

The phone rings, and Katherine, a friend from church, asks how I'm doing. We knew each other years ago but have not really connected again since Larry and I returned to Woodmont. She prefaces the purpose of her call. "I don't know if you are ready to share your experiences with grief yet. I completely understand if you are not, but our ladies' class on Sunday morning is planning a panel discussion on grief and ways to cope. We have three ladies in mind and wonder if you would be willing to be one of the participants. I think you could help us know how to support others suffering through grief."

My first inclination (thinking with my gut and ready to "do" the next thing) to any invitation of this nature is to accept. I am usually comfortable speaking in front of all kinds of groups: students majoring in education, fellow school teachers, or Bible classes. Twice since Jennifer died I have attempted to share in Bible class settings about the loss of our daughter but became too emotional to finish. Both times, I momentarily forgot how hard it might be to share; I just opened my mouth and started talking (my default behavior in most situations).

This invitation allows me time to think before I speak. As she talks, my mind runs through all these considerations, and I finally tell her I need some time to think about it.

Although I often speak of Jennifer when teaching my eighth-graders, as well as with friends and family, this will be different Since I'll be a member of a panel, I think I can manage. I don't have to prepare a full class period or even retell the events of Jennifer's death if I choose not to. I let Katherine know I will accept the invitation, knowing they are looking for practical suggestions in helping others through grief.

My plan is to talk about:

- the shock of her death and the support we received from our church families
- the first year of grief - shock
- little things that helped me or did not help (Psalm 42 which I read so many times)
- the books that helped
- the importance of the holistic plan I made at Trevecca, including prayer and journaling.

When I enter the classroom on the scheduled Sunday, I am welcomed into a group of twenty-five women of all ages. Since I speak last, I try to add new information to the topic. I use my notes to help me focus and then release my constricted lungs in relief as we finish. After class, Lajuana Gill, the wife of our worship minister, introduces herself to me. "My husband, Randy, wrote a song using the words in Psalm 42, as we suffered a different type of grief over our son."

I am thrilled to meet her. "I love that song, "Deep Calls to Deep"[52] and listen to the Zoe album all the time. Thank you for telling me."

I receive encouraging feedback after class and feel good about my part. However, on the way home from church I realize how physically exhausted I am. It takes more out of me than I realize. I'm learning that grieving takes many forms. Even when I am not weeping or despondent over memories, this overwhelming physical exhaustion consumes my energy.

I receive a note during the week from one of the class members. She thanks me for sharing but also shares the "aha" moment for her when she heard this:

> *I find that seeing a close friend is easier for me than a casual friend. The most common question asked is "How are you?" With a close friend, I feel free to be honest: "It's been a hard week." But with a casual friend, questions need to be asked, especially if you have not seen each other lately. Those questions and hugs can trigger emotions for me and the other person.*

My footbridge of faith often has been held up by other people; they give me the strength to step out and share my journey. This first experience of sharing reminds me of the emotional cost of exposing my frayed and hurting places. Despite my desire to help others, I realize, it's too soon. This baby step of courage opened unprotected spaces in my broken heart.

Knowing my experiences in teaching and speaking, people often tell me, "Oh, you will be able to help so many people with grief."

I mentally respond with, "I didn't sign up for this experience. I don't know when or if I'll ever be able to help anyone else."

This I Know Now:

My independent nature sometimes finds it difficult to accept help from others. I've learned to swallow my pride and say "yes" when I need help. For over twenty-two years as a Special Educator, I helped parents of children with disabilities navigate their way through the education system, as well as learn to give their child the wings they needed to be more independent. Helping and supporting others is in my DNA, so the patterns of my life crumbled in my grief. This unfamiliar pathway required humility and acceptance, a journey I took one day at a time.

Now I Am Thankful for:

- the faculty at Trevecca who supported my journey
- my girlfriend circle for always being there when I need them
- learning to follow God's lead in the journey

Your Turn:

- Don't worry about ANYTHING
- Pray about EVERYTHING, especially

_____

- Tell God what I need
- Thank Him for all He has done.

Philippians 4:6-7

> *Then you will experience God's peace, which exceeds anything we can understand. His peace will guard your hearts and minds as you live in Christ Jesus. NLT*

Chapter 15

HOPE

I'll be there to help you carry on,
I will never leave you alone.
— Janet Paschal

August 2004

"Have you ever been white water rafting?" Lora asked.

"No, but I've always wanted to," I answer.

"There is a group from church planning a trip. I'm not real crazy about the water, but maybe it will be fun. Wanna go?"

"Yes! When? How much?" I demand.

The first week in August finds Lora and I headed to southeast Tennessee to float down the Ocoee River. I've never been white water rafting but love to swim. I can't wait to try this the new adventure.

As soon as we commit to the trip, my teacher-brain begins searching for ways to connect this experience to my eighth-graders. I have a Steven Covey video that uses white water as a metaphor for the changes we face in life. He says that if we have a solid core of beliefs and values, we can adjust to the "white water" changes we encounter.[53] I decide to use "Living in a Whitewater World of Change" as a year-long theme to reinforce the importance of having core beliefs before entering the "whitewater" of high school. My personal venture in white water rafting will introduce this theme, making the metaphor more memorable to my students. I can see the bulletin board now, a picture of their "ancient" teacher paddling through white water rapids!

Early one Saturday morning we meet the rest of the group at the church building, carpooling toward southeast Tennessee. After a two-hour drive to Chattanooga, another half an hour north takes us to Cleveland, Tennessee. Finally, the lush green mountains of the Cherokee National Forest surround us. As we near Ducktown, a silver ribbon appears on our right as the lush green of the forest swallows the sun. My heart beats a little faster in anticipation, while Lora's knuckles tighten on the steering wheel, her eyes widen as a gasp escapes, "Ooooh." This adventure is not for the faint of heart, but she does not back down from a challenge.

Once we snap on helmets and life vests, divide into groups of six, and board a big blue school bus, the momentum of the day takes on a life of its own. Rachel, our guide, instructs us on paddling techniques and safety procedures. We scramble into the raft as she pushes us into calm waters. With three of us on each side of the raft and our guide in the back, we dip our paddles in the water and begin. A few minutes of intense paddling finds us headed directly into the river bank. Rachel quickly steers us away from other rafts, and patiently gives us some "special" instruction on paddling *together*. It seems we all had our own ideas about when and how to dip and stroke. Since we are all novices at this, we laugh and try again.

We adapt to the river's rhythm of calm green pools that suddenly turn into rushing white water over hidden boulders. The power and weight of whitewater push the boat wherever it pleases, but Rachel yells commands to us that guide us around boulders and through narrow passages. The human obstacles are just as treacherous as hidden boulders: capsized boats, stalled rafts in our path, or the occasional blue raft stranded on a huge boulder or swamped with water. This adrenaline-filled adventure requires every ounce of focus to remain afloat.

When we come to a gentle, slow-moving section of the river, we drift with the current; I look up at the mountains around us. All at once I realize this is the same dense green thick forest where Jennifer died. Before I left home, Larry reminded me that we would be very close to the Cherokee National Forest, and as usual, my head acknowledged this fact. But I still have not learned that even if my head knows of a situation, my heart-feelings unexpectedly slip forward. I share parts of the story with Lora as we gaze at God's creation.

In the last green stretch of tranquil water, I slip over the side to swim, actually floating since the life jacket make it difficult to swim. Although I love to swim, the water is freezing cold even on a hot day in August; therefore, I am not motivated to stay long! Climbing back in the raft requires more upper body strength than I possess, so I'm grateful for all hands pulling me forward. Please, let there be no pictures!

When we push through Hell Hole, the most challenging rapid, our outfitter company takes a picture of each raft which we will gladly purchase later to document that we fought the mighty Ocoee River.

Today's experience reminds me of some of Jennifer's outdoor adventures as a teenager, jumping cliffs in Jamaica (which I also did, once), mountain climbing in Colorado, as well as two snow skiing trips. Josh introduced her to mountain biking, and they also hiked through the Smokies one winter with Greg.

When I return home, I gather brochures, pictures, stories, and the perfect read-aloud novel for this unit, Gary Paulsen's *The River*. Sorting through our pictures, I take a closer look at Lora and me standing in front of a Ducktown road sign. I can see her collar bones protruding above the neckline of her shirt. When did she get this skinny?

November

Fall Retreat

Another road trip with Lora!

In November the Women's Retreat for Woodmont Hills meets in Monteagle, near Sewanee, TN. We take Lora's car and her extensive alphabetized CD collection. Have I mentioned she's a little OCD?

"I want you to hear this CD by an amazing Christian singer," she tells me. "Her style is unique, sometimes jazzy, and she writes many of her songs. Just listen to this song."

Janet Paschal's mellow tones and simple arrangement grab my attention. When she reaches the chorus, my eyes fill.

And it won't rain always.

The clouds will soon be gone.

The sun that they've been hiding

Has been there all along.

And it won't rain always.

God's promises are true.

The sun's gonna shine in His own good time,

And He will see you through.[54]

And there it was – the Christian music I love but had abandoned after Jennifer's death. That song slid right into my dry broken heart; I can't help but smile. The shield I built around my heart guards my emotions from consuming pain, but these words and this music remind me of truth. Janet's voice gently puts down roots in my soul, a fresh step in the healing process.

When we arrive in Sewanee we drive around the University of the South and finally arrive at St. Mary's Villa, our destination. The view from the mountaintop is stunning, a deep valley surrounded by the smoky rolling Appalachian foothills. I find a place outside to settle on the grass and watch the sunset, enjoying quiet moments of meditation as I reflect on God's power and majesty.

My friend, Joan, prepares a supper of hot soup, fruit, cheese, and crackers. We find our roommates for the night, make our beds in the dorm-style rooms, then talk and snack until we fall asleep.

I always love the close communion I find with sisters in Christ as we spend time in prayer, study, and fellowship, but this retreat is the first for me since Jennifer's death. The weekend's topic is "Living in the Moment". Our schedule provides times to be alone, seeking time with God through a variety of avenues; inside my registration packet, I discover a small, thin book by John Eldredge, *Epic*.

Early Saturday morning I find a quiet place to stretch with some yoga poses and then open *Epic*. The writing immediately captures my English teacher's radar by introducing this spiritual book with the idea of *story*. Madeleine L'Engle, a prolific writer for teens and adults, says, "All of life is a story."[55] I've used this quote and others like it for years with my students as we read literature and analyze the elements of a story.

Eldredge says, "Story is the language of the heart."[56] I begin highlighting these powerful sentences, giving mental high fives and silent "Amen" to page after page. This writer understands *story*. He pulls from the films of our times to explain an epic story. God's story, His pursuit of us, His rescue of us, is an epic story told in Scripture.

Our retreat activities on Saturday morning include some silly games, speakers, and small group time. As my small group gathers outside around a picnic table to pray, Joan gives thanks to God for my ability to laugh again.

Kathy, a member of the girlfriend circle, planned an afternoon hike to Raven Point in the nearby South Cumberland State Park. Ranger Jason, also Kathy's son, meets us for a one-and-a-half-mile climb to the top of a ridge. When we reach Raven's Point, we find a flat limestone ledge and a spectacular overlook. I take in a lung full of air and gaze out over valleys and ridges dressed in brilliant colors.

Once again, I'm looking at Jennifer and Josh country. Unexpected. Breathtaking. Heart-wrenching. And then someone in the group jokes, "Careful, don't step off the edge." And then another wisecrack, another warning about getting too close to the edge.

I back away from the group, slammed with memories of Jennifer's fall in a place just like this. My mind closes, and I turn inward, pushing away the sadness. I'm standing on shaky ground; I need to leave, get away from this danger. I stand off to the side, desperately holding on to self-control and waiting for us to leave.

After our evening meal, we meet for worship with songs and prayer, sharing the Lord's supper. I take the bread and wine with the small group of friends sitting near me.

Lark hugs me with words of encouragement. "I'm so proud of you. Your strength inspires me. I love you."

Deep fissures of emotion well up again; once more my self-control is slipping away. I escape outside, gulping in the cool evening air. I walk around the building, gazing at the clear starry sky. Grasping for emotional control, I finally break down with gut-wrenching pain. Tears I can deal with, but uncontrollable sobbing? No, this is an ugly cry that leaves me drained, exhausted.

Joan finds me. "Can you come back in? We are almost done; I'd like to pray with you."

"Okay. I'll be in soon." Drawing in another lungful of air, sending silent prayers for peace and calm for my soul.

When worship is over, the group heads outside for a bonfire. Lora and I pack her car to drive back to Nashville since we planned to spend only one night at the retreat. On the long drive back, I replay the weekend in my head. Lora matches my silence; she reads me well and knows the emotional roller coaster has depleted my energy.

Baby Steps

Later in November my nephew's wedding is scheduled for Thanksgiving weekend. The last wedding I attended was Brad and Becky's in May of 2003. Since then I have avoided all weddings to guard my heart against memories and pain.

Could I attend a wedding of a family member without all the emotional turmoil I experienced in 2003? I chose not to attend another nephew's wedding in the spring of 2004; memories of leaving a wedding weeping provide a vivid reminder of emotional landmines. I view Andrew's wedding as a test. With support from my brothers and their wives, I decide to travel with family to Arkansas for the wedding. Helping decorate for the rehearsal dinner provides a distraction. I thank God my heart remains stable throughout all the activities. The only side effects? A tense, tight neck, which is my body's typical reaction to stress. After a quick chiropractic adjustment from one of the guests, I am able to relax.

In December I take my first step toward active participation in church activities. I read Scripture with Larry during morning worship. This qualifies as a major First Step in more than one way: we lead the entire congregation (from the stage). Our church tradition does not allow women to take a leadership role in public worship, but the elders for the Woodmont church are known for careful reconsideration of some long-held policies. For several years women have participated in a variety of roles in public worship at this church. I confess my nervousness came from a double-edged sword: leading in worship and taking this first step back to active participation in the church. Having Larry up front on the stage with me provides emotional support, so all goes well.

One other event of note as 2004 comes to an end: we receive Josh's family Christmas newsletter with pictures and news of their three children. Josh is pictured with a lovely young woman with long blond hair. No caption or explanation is included. My inference? Josh is dating again.

January 29, 2005

Sleepover

After school on Friday I dash home to throw pajamas, toothbrush, and a little makeup into an overnight bag. With directions from Belinda, I head south on I65 to Spring Hill for our annual Girlfriend Sleepover. Nashville traffic on a Friday evening is frustrating. Since I live on the north side of town, my route takes me around downtown and then into the mass of traffic heading south for Cool Springs, Brentwood, and Franklin.

Almost an hour later I finally find Belinda's house. "You didn't tell me to pack a lunch for this trip to your house!" I tell her when she greets me at the door. Everyone but Carrie, who is in Rugby, has already arrived. We order pizza, enjoy the comfort food, and dig into a rich chocolate cake Lark brought.

After I read my journal aloud from last year's sleepover, we each share the highlights of our year: family, work, personal struggles. This year Kathy lost her father, joining Joan and me in that empty feeling when both parents die. Lark's oldest, Neil, has been stationed in Bagdad for almost a year.

This time of reflection with friends who have walked together through some mountaintop experiences, as well as some dark valleys, provides each of us time to look at our lives, often through the eyes of another. Joan says I have blossomed this year. I don't recognize a change, but my principal recently said something similar. He observed that Lora brought my smile back.

I read aloud the acknowledgments I wrote in my dissertation, thanking the many people who walked the footbridge of faith with me through the process of earning my doctorate. Each woman in this group is named, and tonight they all toast me for my progress in this journey. We sit up until we can't stay awake any longer.

A rainy, gray Saturday morning greets us the next day. After breakfast we form our prayer huddle, praying for each other, for our children and spouses. After hugs and well wishes, some of us head to College Grove to Joan's antique store. Her frequent trips to New England add to her stock; clearly, she has fallen in love with the area and is planning a trip for us to New England in June.

This I Know Now:

In this season of my journey, I felt as though I was emerging from a dark cocoon where I had lain, curled inside with clenched fists. Despite the darkness, I never felt alone; I know God lived in the darkness with me, suffered with me. I look back on many of these events with fond memories, despite times of gut-wrenching pain. The day on the river with Lora brought such delight; participating in worship opened the cocoon for light to stream in.

Now I Am Thankful for:

- Janet Paschal's music and words that touched my wounded soul
- the comfort found with lifelong friends
- sharing adventures and retreats with Lora
- discovering John Eldredge and his writing

Your Turn:

- Don't worry about ANYTHING
- Pray about EVERYTHING
- Tell God what I NEED, not what I want

- THANK Him for all He has done.

Philippians 4:6-7

> *Then you will experience God's peace, which exceeds anything we can understand. His peace will guard your hearts and minds as you live in Christ Jesus. NLT*

Chapter 16

HOLDING ON

"I'll say to myself, 'You're loved.
Your pain is God's pain.
Go ahead and embrace the struggle
and chaos of it all, the splendor
the messiness, the wonder, the agony
the joy, the conflict. Love all of it.'"
—Sue Monk Kidd[57]

January 2005

Lora and I join the Woodmont choir which was formed to sing at the Easter service. We spend Wednesday nights together, leaving school every Wednesday afternoon, driving across town, grabbing tacos for a quick supper, singing, and then driving back to Donelson. Lora's car fills with laughter on these trips as we rehash the school day. Learning new music provides a creative outlet separate from teaching; laughter and singing furnish new distractions for me.

February 2005

A New Support Group

Last fall Lora's battle with anorexia became obvious to more people. The more time we spend together, the more I learn about how this condition controls every part of her life. I feel out of my depth with her condition, so I mainly listen when she wants to talk. She calls me on a Saturday morning to tell me her racing heart scares her. Lora asks me to go with her to see a counselor that morning.

After the counselor hears some of her story, he agrees to begin sessions with her; however, she must first go to the ER immediately to get her heart checked out. After a few tests, the doctor suggests that her heart problem is likely due to all the caffeine she consumes from her always-present coffee cup; she needs to cut back on caffeine. I feel like we make a little progress by at least getting her to see a counselor, but I wonder if she will follow up with more sessions.

When Lora joined the praise team at church she developed a close friendship with LaJuana, the director's wife. LaJuana recognizes Lora's problem right away and asks Lora point-blank if she is anorexic. Lora answers her honestly in the affirmative, so when LaJuana questions, "Are you ready to address the problem?" Lora agrees she needs help and is ready. LaJuana has experience counseling young women with eating disorders and gathers a small support group including my friend, Lark, LaJuana, and me. Vera joins us later.

The group meets every Tuesday night at the Woodmont church building; LaJuana carefully leads Lora through some painful memories in her life. She focuses on spiritual issues such as feelings of inadequacy, unworthiness, and a negative view of God. As she guides Lora through a variety of exercises to resolve many issues, Lark and I provide moral and spiritual support, even some roleplaying. I begin to understand some of her issues and am so thankful I see some progress.

April

On the anniversary date of Jennifer's death, Emalie and I each take a personal day from work and spend it at Cheekwood, a beautiful estate filled with gardens and a refurbished mansion. We take our time, enjoying a relaxed day with no time constraints. The diversion keeps my thoughts from straying to sad memories. In the evening I receive several phone calls from friends, just to let me know they are thinking of me and praying for me. One of the teenage girls from Jennifer's teen group from the Cookeville church calls and tells me about her difficulties all day as she remembers Jennifer. She reflects on Jennifer's influence on her spiritual and emotional life. Her stories lift my spirit.

Courtney also calls tonight with news about Josh – he is engaged. She wants me to know before I hear it from someone else. Since Josh moved to Middle Tennessee he has not called, but perhaps he was not ready to tell us he was getting married. A few days later Josh does call to let us know of his engagement; I invite him to come and see us anytime, but the conversation is brief. Thinking about his marriage pulls up more deep-seated feelings than I expect, especially on this day.

In respect to Larry's desire for privacy, the story of my journey of grief has not included much about Larry's thoughts or our conversations together. We cope with our grief in totally different ways, just as my extrovert traits and his introvert traits often find us dealing with all kinds of issues in opposite ways. But I need his quiet presence. He never presses me or insists on a conversation about my emotions or state of mind.

June

New Adventures

My first and only venture into teaching at the college level begins and ends with two weekends in June. I teach two separate groups of Masters' level students a literacy course. I love this subject and spend hours researching and preparing, but the barriers and logistics of teaching long hours, moving classrooms (and all my teaching materials) with no time to give adequate feedback to students on their work cause me to reconsider college teaching. Perhaps immature eighth graders and I are a better fit.

As soon as the last college-level class ends I catch a plane to New Hampshire to join a group of women Joan has gathered for a week of touring New England. We visit the rocky coast of Maine, get our feet wet in the icy waters of the Atlantic, marvel at church buildings and cemeteries from the 1600s, and take pictures of each other surrounded by fields of brilliant purple lupines. We eat fresh lobster and blueberry pie in Maine, pancakes and homemade fudge in Vermont. All of us loved roaming through antique stores and tourist shops. We watch *On Golden Pond* one night reminding me of the unique sound of loons. The next day three of us trek through woods filled with biting black flies to find a loon nesting at the edge of a lake. Lark and I connect all these experiences into ways to teach language arts to our students in the fall. The rest of the group did their best to hide their eyerolls at our irritating excitement.

October

Remembering

The class of 1965 at Southside High School holds their 40th reunion this month; a phone call from a classmate encourages me to attend my first union. I drive to Gadsden, Alabama for the weekend, unsure of what to expect. Although I only attended one year at this school, our class of 38 enabled me to fit easily into the culture. When I arrive, I don't recognize anyone, so I scan nametags. Soon I find myself pulled into a group and catch up on what each one is doing with their life, but as the evening progresses my excitement fades, reality sets in; I'm the newcomer, again. Many class members still live in this small community and know each other well. Expectations meet reality when I realize tonight's agenda is dedicated to honoring the football coach. The "football" boys control the after-dinner speeches; how could I forget the focus of the culture of our school: football and basketball, guys only?

I wanted to hear everybody's story, what happened after graduation, who married who, professional careers. The few stories I hear make me realize I have little in common with most of the people here and most are not interested in my story.

Despite my disappointment in the reunion, I have places to find and people to see. Before the reunion, I drive around Wharton's Bend and Etowah Park to find our old houses. Each place brought back memories: which school I attended, the ages of my brothers at each house, the trees I climbed, and gardens I helped plant. The farms in the Bend display cotton fields ready for harvest, dark brown plants bursting full of soft white cotton.

Sunday morning, I attend the church where Daddy preached for several years on Rainbow Drive. I meet a few friends from those days and then go to lunch with the Keenums; our families camped together, shared a garden, and many family celebrations. Daddy and Curt, two good ol' country boys, loved raising bird dogs and spent many fall mornings bird hunting.

Sitting on the couch in their den, I remember when they remodeled their house and added this den. Curt and Louise sit on each side of me to see the album of pictures I have of Jennifer. As I tell her story, their sadness and support touch me, and I think, "This is how I would introduce Jennifer as a young woman to Mama and Daddy." I see my daughter through the eyes of these two people who loved my parents, my family and in turn, my daughter. Curt's big hand softly rests on my shoulder; tears leak from my eyes. Curt is a man with few words and seldom shows his emotions.

As my car heads north to Tennessee, I take several cleansing breaths. This weekend dragged me back down to my closet of pain. I thought that door was firmly shut. My head tricked me into believing this trip would be fun; I was sure my heart was carefully guarded against this wave of feelings. Once again, unexpected grief threatens.

November 12

Woodmont Women's Retreat

LaJuana, Lora, and I ride to the retreat in Monteagle, talking and laughing the whole trip. LaJuana is the keynote speaker for this retreat; her topic: "Sabbath Rest".

Saturday morning the three of us gather early in the meeting room to help LaJuana with her technology. Her PowerPoint is critical to the presentation, so Lora and I sit on the front row, just in case. LaJuana leads us through a study of God's intention for us in finding rest for our spiritual, emotional, physical, and mental well-being. Our packets contain journals and we spend time writing about a phrase from Psalm 63:1-5, "in the shadow of your wings."

My journal entry:

> I feel wings hovering and surrounding me. They are in my peripheral vision — just there. I can see the shadows more clearly than the wings. I am comforted and find peace with the knowledge of God. His Son and Spirit are supporting me when I walk in the valley.

LaJuana introduces us to some ancient practices, forms of worship completely foreign to the tradition of our church. Our church heritage emphasizes Biblical knowledge and memorizing Scripture. The practices of the rosary, the Divine Office, and repeating prayers from a book were a mystery to me. LaJuana prepares us for meditation and silence before we spend time in silence.

During the first break, the woman sitting next to me asks me if I am comfortable talking about the loss of Jennifer. We knew each other years ago but have not seen each other since Jennifer's death. I give her the short version of Jennifer's death, not realizing I was stepping on a booby trap. I try to finish the conversation as my emotions build, excusing myself as soon as possible. I had to escape the ocean of feelings welling up in my chest. Our conversation along with the singing, prayers, and meditation of the morning cause intense aching in my soul. Once again, I thought my heart had been carefully protected. The strong need to escape allows me some physical space to compose myself and calm my racing heart.

I quietly sit on a back row when I return to the next session, participating, but guarding my heart. I gather my things later from the front row, so my friend doesn't know I was upset. She did not cause my emotions; my conflict is between my head and heart. I could have avoided the whole conversation by just declining to share, but I seldom fail to share when asked. My natural inclination has always been to open my mouth first and then think.

Now that inclination gets me into emotional trouble.

After lunch Lora, LaJuana, and I explore the campus of the University of the South. The beautiful All Saints Chapel of the Episcopal Church provides a quiet place to continue our morning contemplations. I pick up some great little pamphlets that give me more tools for meditation, and I tuck them inside my journal.

Before dinner LaJuana encourages us to find some time to meditate or pray. I slip inside the tiny empty retreat chapel, lit by candles but freezing cold.

I feel the intensity of caring for the emotional, spiritual, and mental lives of my eighth graders. But by sitting still, slowing my breath, silence encircles me. Tension releases from my body despite the cold.

The days ahead crowd my thoughts with memories of Jennifer once more;

in thirteen days her birthday arrives. Then Thanksgiving and Christmas.

I move to the front altar and kneel, holding the beads LaJuana gave us. I repeat the phrase: "LORD JESUS, HAVE MERCY ON ME" ten times and emphasize LORD. The next ten repetitions emphasize JESUS. My prayer follows this pattern, stressing a different word each time.

Next, I pray for my family, friends, the church, Jennifer, the world. Then in complete surrender, I lay all my burdens at the cross. The anguish inside my soul breaks open, and I weep, my sobs breaking the silence in the chapel. I cry until nothing is left, but something has changed. The gut-wrenching emotions earlier today overpowered my tenuous self-control. Tonight, leaving my burdens at the cross soothes the broken places in me.

I make my way to the dining room where everyone is waiting for the doors to open. When I join my friends, their conversations give me a moment to reflect on the last half hour. I quietly tell them my experience in the chapel and how refreshed I feel. These sweet girlfriends immediately gather around me in support. Joan says it was worth the whole retreat for me to experience this lifting of my burden.

Before we leave the retreat, Lora and I write in each other's journals.

Lora's entry in my journal:

Martell

I am continually amazed by the surprises God brings me. It's so hard to believe how my life has changed since I met you. I would hate to imagine where I would be without you.

I know these events are always somewhat painful for you, and I know we both avoid the touchy-feely things... but I am so glad you came, and I hope you are as well. I was so happy to hear that you were refreshed today. I have hoped for that for you.

I hope you know just how much I love you and am so thankful that God brought you into my life. I have been so blessed by you. I feel like I have family right down the hall at work, and you have introduced me to my spiritual family (not to mention my "support group"). I have so much fun with you — it's fun to get lost sometimes along the journey!

I love you!

Lora

The car fills with laughter on our trip home when we discover we are driving south instead of north on the interstate.

This I Know Now:

Lora's support group, our time at choir practice, and her friendship made a significant difference in my perspective.

The tools I learned and used to practice meditation, the Jesus Prayer, and *The Ransomed Heart* gave me a foundation for drawing nearer to God, even though I totally neglected all these tools in the next year.

I felt the presence of Jesus when I spent time in the little chapel at the Women's Retreat.

Now I am Thankful for:

- time in the chapel that led to healing
- the tools LaJuana introduced at the retreat
- time with the Keenums in Gadsden

Your Turn:

- Don't worry about ANYTHING
- Pray about EVERYTHING

- Tell God what I NEED
  - THANK Him for all He has done.
  - In my circumstance today, I may not be able to see His gifts and blessings, but I can find at least three blessings today.

  _____

  _____

  _____

Philippians 4:6-7

> *Then you will experience God's peace, which exceeds anything we can understand. His peace will guard your hearts and minds as you live in Christ Jesus. NLT*

Chapter 17
LETTING GO

There is no getting over death,
only learning how to travel alongside it.
—Sandra Cisneros[58]

Discovering Tools I Need

Immediately after the retreat I begin a concentrated effort to establish the practices learned over the weekend. Following Jennifer's death, I made a quiet time with God a priority but fell out of the habit, especially during the busy-ness of school. My journal after the retreat is filled with notes as I search and experiment with different tools.

November 14, 2005,

The Sacred Way by Tony Jones[59]

"My Journey of Meditation, Chapter 3"

- Thoughts on silence and solitude: being quiet and alone make us better, more personal, more Christ-centered.
- By focusing on this short verse and repeating it, it feels like I am talking to God.

"And if I wander off like a lost sheep — seek me! I'll recognize you by the sound of your voice."

Psalm 119:176. MSG

November 17

"Sacred Reading, Chapter 4"

Jones suggests using a Bible such as *The Message* that is unmarked (a new idea to me). Then choose a text to meditate such as Psalm 119. Repeat it slowly aloud.

This morning Larry reminds me that Jennifer would be 25 today. Where would she be today? What would she be doing? I talk about her with my students in class today, and the legacy she left.

November 18

Lora's Condo with LaJuana, Vera, and Lark

Lora invites her support group over to her house on Friday night — a sleepover for some of us. We admire her new dining room set as she gives us a tour of the place. We stop in Lora's bedroom a few minutes to chat. LaJuana comes out of the bathroom, dazed, wide eyes, and touching her throat. She points to a frame on the bathroom wall and questions Lora, "Where did you get that?"

Lora peeks in to see the frame and says, "Martell gave it to me."

"Those are my words from a girls' retreat!" LaJuana exclaims as she stares at me.

I had no idea who said those words. I explain, "Jennifer brought that sign home from a retreat at the Madison church when she was in high school. When I cleaned out Jennifer's closet, I tucked it away, saving for someone or some occasion. Not long ago, thinking of Lora, I remembered it; I framed it and gave it to her."

The frame held these words:

APPEARING TO BE

PERFECT IS DECEPTIVE

and

being beautiful and skinny

doesn't last very long;

but a young woman who

trusts in the Lord

is Loved.

We all look at each other in silence and consider the path of those words, from LaJuana to Jennifer, to me, and to Lora.

Chill bumps.

God-moves-in-mysterious-ways moment.

LaJuana calls it an electric moment.

Our conversation flows around this amazing working of God through many lives. I share pieces of Jennifer's story with LaJuana and Vera. These friends make it easy for me to talk about her, even in this emotional moment; they fill me with love and support.

November 24, Thanksgiving Day

My study in *The Sacred Way* reinforces LaJuana's teaching on the Jesus Prayer.

The practice of the "Jesus Prayer," also known as the Centering Prayer, suggests a place of absolute silence, perhaps a dimly lit room. Begin the practice by bowing the head so the mind descends into the heart for breath; focus on breathing and begin the prayer with the rhythm of breath. Breathe in: "Lord Jesus Christ" and breathe out: "have mercy on me."

I choose the word "peace," settle down, close my eyes, and hold the word.

When thoughts wander, I return to "peace." I sit in the stillness and come out of the silence in prayer.

November 25

I'm ready to come home to worship, devotion, and study time. The retreat inspired me to make these new practices part of my quiet time. I prepare a Sacred Space in Jennifer's room using her Blessing Chest, a chest we gave her when she turned 18. I cover it with a green tablecloth, add a green lamp and a wooden tray of candles, shells, and potpourri. I place a basket of Bibles, journals, pens, and matches beside the tray. On the floor is Jennifer's sheepskin rug and a big basket of the books I have collected in my studies. Last, I add Mama's ladder-back chair.

November 26

I find this prayer in the Daily Office and immediately copy it in my journal.

Keep watch dear Lord with those who
work or
watch or
weep this night
and give your angels charge over those who sleep.
Tend the sick, Lord Jesus Christ:
give rest to the weary
bless the dying
soothe the suffering,
pity the afflicted,
shield the joyous,
and all for your love's sake, Amen.

from The Book of Common Prayer[60]

November 27

I review all my journals and notes since Jennifer died. I read some psalms in *The Message,* but I miss the rich language of other versions. I look for a Scripture of praise since my journals are filled with my cries for mercy. Psalm

31:22 seems appropriate:

> *"But you heard my prayer*
> *When I cried out to you for help." NCV*

Psalm 40 appears to meet my needs today.

> *I waited patiently for the Lord; he turned to me and heard my cry.*
> *He lifted me out of the slimy pit, out of the mud and mire;*
> *He set my feet on a rock and gave me a firm place to stand.*
> *He put a new song in my mouth, a song of praise to our God.*
> *Many people will see and fear the Lord and put their trust in him.*

December 10

A trip to Lifeway bookstore always gives me inspiration; I discover two new books: *The Ransomed Heart*[61] by John Eldredge, and *Through a season of grief*[62] by Bill Dunn and Kathy Leonard. The chapter titles of their book pull me in – "When your dreams fall apart."

Christmas

The fourth Christmas since Jennifer died finally feels like time for putting up a Christmas tree. Since we usually picked out a real tree together when Jennifer was alive, I thought an artificial one would be better. I buy a small tree for school for my teacher decorations, a small 60's silver tree for the landing on the stairs, and a tall green one for the front bay window.

I pull out Christmas boxes for decorating and decide to create a Memory Tree out of the living room tree, using Jennifer's annual ornaments, Mama's ornaments, and others we collected through the years. Sorting through ornaments brings no sad feelings, but as I hang them on the tree, grief slips in. Not the devastating depression (on the couch, no feelings) but enough to linger over on Monday and Tuesday.

If I dwell on ornaments or pictures, I am sure to feel blue. I eventually clear out the big boxes and put them upstairs, so I can use my meditation and yoga space again. I've neglected meditation this week; it's time to recharge.

December 19

I'm still searching for a routine for meditation; over the next few days I use several of the books in my collection:

- *The Sacred Way*
- Tools: The Daily Office, Jesus Prayer, Centering Prayer
- *Through a Season of Grief*
- *The Ransomed Heart*
- *The Divine Hours: Prayers for Autumn and Wintertime*[63]

The Ransomed Heart

This book soon becomes one of my favorites; it contains readings from several of Eldredge's other books. I am gaining a new perspective on God's role in our lives in this book. Eldredge contends that instead of viewing God as the Author of the Story we are living, we should think of him as the central character in the larger story. God is not the Mastermind, like Oz; he is IN our story as the hero.[64] He comes to save us, but like all good stories, the hero shows up at the last minute. My heart begins to meditate on this totally new idea for me.

*You will seek me and find me
when you seek me with all your heart.*

Jeremiah 29:13 NIV

I find this new understanding speaking to me: to find God, I need to look for Him with all my heart. To hear His voice, I need to listen with all my heart. To love Him, I need to love with all my heart. Without my heart, I cannot have life.[65]

My book is filled with highlight underlining; I fill a journal with notes, and then I reread these one-page passages. The battle my heart and head have been waging begins to make sense through Eldredge's teaching.

2006

Wandering in the Wilderness

January through May, my journal contains no notes from daily Bible reading, prayer, or reflections. Besides neglecting meditation, my indifference includes exercise. No swimming all spring. A winter of neglecting my soul.

An aimless feeling shuts down motivation, wandering without purpose but not depressed. On April 13, the anniversary of Jennifer's death, I take the day off and my friend, Liz and I go to lunch. Her breast cancer has returned to her back, lungs, and bones, so I want to spend some time with her. She looks good right now, and her pain is improving. Focusing on someone else provides the distraction I need on this day.

May 2006

A dark depression slams me the weekend of Mother's Day. Josh and Jennifer planned their wedding date to be May 2003. I don't know why that thought comes up after four years. Looking at a picture of her and Josh, sadness pours into my chest.

At the end-of-the-year school awards, I present the third Jennifer Souder Humanitarian Award to Addison. She reminds me of a butterfly; it fits her personality, and she just makes me smile.

As school ends I plan my summer projects to paint and redecorate the kitchen, bathroom, and living room.

June 22, 2006

I begin again with a daily morning meditation, swimming first and then a quiet time on the bench by the pond.

Today's reading in Isaiah 30:18-21 contains sweet consolation for me:

The Lord wants to show His mercy. He will comfort me.
The Lord is a fair God.
Everyone who waits for His help will be happy.
The Lord hears my crying and will comfort me.

When He hears me, He will help me.
The Lord gave me sorrow and hurt like the
bread and water I eat every day.
He is my teacher, and He will not hide from me.
I will see my teacher with my own eyes.
If I go the wrong way – to the right or to the left,
I will hear a voice behind me saying,
"This is the right way. You should go this way." NCV

July 8, 2006

I greet each morning this summer with regular meditation and study. *The Ransomed Heart* engages me as much as Chamber's *Utmost*. The mystery of God's sovereignty and man's free will continues to challenge my thoughts – this has been a continual struggle for me over Jennifer's death.

Last week was spent completing projects and sorting through boxes of pictures. When some of Jennifer's pictures appear, my heart jumps. Hidden triggers once again!

Later in the Summer

"The ultimate risk for anyone to take is to love."[66] C. S. Lewis simplifies the problem of broken hearts with this solution: "Love anything and heart will be wrung and/or broken. To keep heart intact --- give it to NO ONE, not even an animal."[67] But I know there is always a steadfast God!

December 2006

The holiday blues have set in. As often happens, on the last day of the semester, after all the parties and parting wishes, I feel empty and sad. Nothing to look forward to, no plans for Christmas.

The Friday after Christmas, I find myself deep-sighing, a reminder of sadness, but not debilitating depression. Unmotivated to even call anybody - just content to be a slug. Reading lots of fiction, Nora Roberts and Luanne Rice. I must be careful with Rice's books; I can be surprised by the intense emotions her characters prompt from me. I work a little every day on my plan for the second semester.

At the end of 2006, I find myself spiritually wandering in the wilderness, hardly looking for water. Physically, I am a couch potato, not swimming or doing yoga.

January 2007

The depression during the holidays has lifted; I find new energy to pay attention to my heart, mind, body, and soul. My journals remain empty, but I make a brief list of thanks this month. One of my students writes me a letter, thanking me for the help I give her at school. It reminds me of one the reasons I teach. I thank God for the many students who want to learn, and the internal drive God gives me to think of "one more" strategy to try with reluctant and disengaged students.

February 2007

Paradigm Shift #1

On Groundhog Day each February Junior Achievement sponsors our local Job Shadow Day when we take eighth graders to a workplace for experiencing real jobs. I accompany a group to the Opryland Hotel for their assignments. With students scattered throughout this sprawling complex, I walk more than usual; by the end of the day, I am limping. Something is wrong with my right foot.

The podiatrist's diagnosis: arthritis in the arch. Since I already take Celebrex for pain in my hands, there is not much more to take for the pain. I get orthotics for my shoes which helps a little. I see a rheumatologist, but this is not rheumatoid arthritis. By spring I am wearing a walking boot on my foot to ease the pain and sitting as much as possible.

June 2007

Paradigm Shift #2

Since 2004 I have experienced severe allergic reactions (hives, gastric distress) and now carry an EpiPen. I know I am allergic to all milk products but continue to have reactions. I finally see an allergist who draws blood to determine other food allergies.

My phone rings one morning just as I pull into a parking space of a high school for an all-day workshop. The nurse confirms the milk allergy, but then she adds, "You are also allergic to wheat. That allergy is more severe than the milk. You are allergic to the protein in milk, not the lactose, and the protein in wheat, not the gluten."

I sit in my car trying to comprehend the impact of this news. My allergic reactions have been so severe lately that I know I must eliminate all the wheat in my diet. I cannot believe it. I love bread, and crackers, and cookies, and pizza, and pasta. Our box lunches provided today will be filled with items I cannot eat! All day I try to wrap my head around this paradigm shift in my life.

After the workshop, I drive to the nearest Whole Foods store to look for some alternatives. Walking the aisles, I look at cereal – no more Bran Flakes. Crackers? I can't find any. I keep walking until I realize my eyes are filling with tears. I quickly leave, sit in my car, and cry. Poor me! Then I wipe my tears and return to the store.

Surprisingly, I find alternatives; even better, I find cookbooks with recipes. Little did I know the impact of a wheat and dairy-free diet in my life. Every outing to a restaurant becomes a challenge. I slowly begin to understand the multitude of ways my food can be contaminated with wheat or milk products in the cooking, especially in a restaurant. I try many new products and recipes in search of substitutes for cookies or bread.

When school ended this year, Lora decided to leave teaching and take a full-time position as a nanny. Since the middle school music position is not guaranteed each year, she decided to end each year's questionable future and go a different direction. I understand her frustration but will desperately miss our close connection during the school day. Even though she lives in our school's neighborhood, her new job is across town.

Paradigm #1

In October 2007 my orthopedic podiatrist determines from a bone density scan and an MRI, I have three stress fractures in my foot due to a bunion and the way I have been walking to minimize my pain. The best solution for arthritis in my arch is to fuse the arch. In December he performs extensive outpatient surgery: a pin for one of the fractures, removal of the bunion, using a bone from my leg to repair the bunion, and fusion of the arch.

I have eight long weeks of recuperation ahead of me.

January 2008

During recuperation time after foot surgery, someone brings us a meal --- so thoughtful, but I stand in the kitchen crying after she leaves because I cannot eat any of it. My food allergies, again. Larry kindly asks, "Will it help if I don't eat it?" But I don't want him to miss out on these home-cooked vegetables.

Lark and Belinda come over one day to make oatmeal cookies using my wheat and dairy-free recipe. They are a riot in my kitchen!

Lark marvels, "You have more than one set of measuring spoons!"

"Of course," I answered. Clearly, neither of these friends spend much time baking in the kitchen. With my instructions they are able to make my favorite recipe plus cheer me with their crazy antics.

During those weeks of sitting and healing, I think of how I longed for a quiet time to meditate, pray, and write. But I cannot or do not (I'm not sure which one), even though I have the time. I primarily read fiction and watch HGTV. I probably have a mild state of depression.

Very few entries can be found in my journal for 2007; health issues seemed to consume my energy and motivation.

This I Know Now:

- Our small support group for Lora helped all of us.
- Christmas will always have the possibility of landmines but most of the years since 2005 have been good ones.

- Depression is always with me, even today. I continue to take medication and pay attention to triggers that can bring about more episodes. I now see a psychiatric nurse practitioner who helps me plan and think through ways to avoid the worst episodes. Medication does not cure depression, but it has helped me.

- Psalm 40 has become one of my favorite passages; I've memorized the first section because I look back on these times as being in a slimy pit, full of mud and muck. My God lifted me out and put my feet on a rock, a firm place to stand.

Now I Am Thankful for:

- all the tools I gathered to use in meditation
- after ten years with food allergies I am now allergy-free! Praise God!
- being able to eat hot rolls, ice cream, monkey bread (2018)

Your Turn:

- Don't worry about ANYTHING, even

- Pray about EVERYTHING
- Tell God what I need
- Thank Him for all He has done.

Philippians 4:6-7

Then you will experience God's peace, which exceeds anything we can understand. His peace will guard your hearts and minds as you live in Christ Jesus. NLT

Chapter 18

SHOCK

*We all need counseling; Jesus sent
the Holy Spirit to be our Counselor.*
—John Eldredge

2008

If you push aside my shirts and pants in the bottom of my closet, you'll find a collection of orthopedic equipment: a large boot for the right foot, a rolling walker, old ace bandages, orthotic shoe inserts, Dr. Scholl's shoe inserts, and several pairs of shoes I cannot wear with orthotics.

My kitchen pantry now contains rice, sorghum, tapioca, and potato flour. The shelf of cookbooks is stuffed with new cookbooks filled with gluten-free and dairy-free recipes. In the trash you can probably find yet another loaf of homemade yeast bread not fit to eat, the result of my constant search for a good-tasting yeast bread made without wheat flour.

The year 2007 reminds me of chronic pain and adjusting to a lifestyle without wheat and milk. Each day I drove to school on as many four-lane roads as possible so I could use the cruise control and save my foot from pressure. I taught sitting on my stool in the front of the classroom and walked as little as possible. Each afternoon and evening found me on the couch with the right foot on piles of pillows while I planned lessons and graded papers.

Recovery after my December surgery seemed endless, so by February, I am eager to return to school.

February

When I learn of the death one of our teachers' adult son, I made a point to locate Allen to offer my sympathy. We shared pieces of our stories and whenever we pass in the hall, one of us asks, "How are you doing today?" Some days our answers are, "Not so good." Other days, "I'm okay." We do not speak often but seem to have an understanding without words. I give him a copy of *When There Are No Words,* and we find a common language. This is the first time I've reached out to offer comfort to someone over the death of their child.

Spring 2008

Jennifer's death date finds me in a pit of despair, but the end of the school year marks a new sadness over the separation of my eighth-grade team. All but one of the teachers on my team are transferring to other schools, a major shift in the dynamics of my work environment. This team stood beside me in front of Jennifer's casket, while holding on to each other. They all knew Jennifer from the days she came to school with me during in-service. I will miss them. The eighth-grade team now has only two of us from the original five, Martha and me.

June 2008

Mild depression continues; allergic reactions from food continue. I think I'm still sad that my life has been limited in my food choices, but at least progress has been made at home – a major clean-out of closets for a yard sale. Summer days give me time to reflect, and I realize this year has been isolating with the long recovery after foot surgery, but also because I often choose not to be part of activities. I seldom call anyone.

It's time to make some changes by adding:

- regular devotion time
- continue daily yoga
- decide on a new church home (we've been visiting churches

closer to home)

- make plans with friends
- put some structure in my day during the summer

I begin morning devotions again with *The Ransomed Heart.* My journal contains notes of some important truths:

> *I won't see clearly what has happened to me, or how to live forward from here UNLESS I see it as a battle, a war against my heart. God appears to abandon me. If I don't come to terms with the WAR, I will believe that God's will allows terrible things to happen to me.*[68]

> *Paul says in 2 Corinthians 4:16 that we do not lose heart. And then he tells us how to not lose heart: fix our eyes not on what is seen, but what is unseen. (NIV)*[69] *If I can look at life in this way, I can live from the heart, no matter what happens.*

And then this statement surprises me:

"The story of my life is the story of a long and brutal assault on my heart by the one who knows what I could be and fears it."[70] Eldredge says the Enemy (Satan) fears the glory in my life that comes from God, and he is hell-bent on destroying it before I act on it.

These thoughts give me much meat to digest.

August 2008

When I have my annual check-up with my gynecologist, we discuss my depression. Even though I see her only once a year, we always discuss Jennifer. She delivered Jennifer, even saw Jennifer once as a patient when Jennifer ran track at Tech. I can count on a sympathetic ear and wise counsel from Dr. Chambers. When I relate the problems of the past year: my foot surgery, difficulties with food allergies, along with a difficult school year, the contributing factors to depression are obvious.

Since I have difficulty in swallowing the Wellbutrin, I cut my pills in half.

She says I am losing its benefits because this an extended release pill, so she increases the dosage and changes the prescription. Another factor I did not even know about!

September 15, 2008

A tragic accident kills the son of one of my co-workers over the weekend. Diane works part-time as a consultant for our school in an office directly across the hall from me. Her son was in a golf cart at a local golf course when a huge tree suddenly fell on top of him.

On Tuesday, I cannot get out of the bed. I work Wednesday and half day on Thursday, but by lunchtime Thursday I cannot contain my tears. Several teachers tell me they will cover my afternoon classes and order me to go home. I leave early Thursday and stay home on Friday.

This bout of depression feels as serious as the first depression of November 2002; I think the combination of losing the full benefits of Wellbutrin and trauma flashback of a friend losing an adult child gives me a double whammy. Everyone at school is so supportive. My teammate, Martha, shields me from obstacles in my way when I'm not even aware of it. The new teachers to our team are young and eager but have been very sensitive to my needs.

October 2008

This year's Girlfriends' annual weekend is a trip to Rugby, TN. Carrie has a second home there and has been trying to get us to come for some time. I meet a carload of the girlfriends after school on Friday, and we head east. We drive two and a half hours east and then north to the Upper Cumberland area. They have a beautiful house set in the woods; Carrie gives us a grand tour of her lovely home, full of antiques from Will's and her family. We linger over dinner and breakfast catching up on everyone's news. Saturday, we tour the restored Rugby village of Victorian homes and buildings. What a great weekend to be away with good friends!

Thanksgiving, 2008

I awaken with a concrete block on my chest. Why Lord? Will this depression never end? Maybe it's the timing - just after Jennifer's birthday, or maybe because I'm not seeing any of my brothers and their families on this holiday.

After visiting many churches in our part of town, we returned to our Madison church home, the place where Jennifer grew up and where we held her funeral. We sit in different places in the three thousand seat auditorium each service, usually near people we don't know. Sometimes I feel emotional during a service, and other times not. The first service we were back, Nila (the friend who came the night we learned of Jennifer's death) found me and held me in a tight hug. I still need to be anonymous while adjusting once again to this familiar church home with all its memories of Jennifer. We usually attend the first service which is more traditional and fine with me. The second service often makes me more emotional.

Christmas 2008

One day before our Christmas break, Diane, the school counselor, comes to me in the hall. Her worried face makes me wonder if a student needs me, but no, Allen is crying in her office and asking for me. I quickly respond, "I know what this is about. His son died last February."

Diane is so surprised, "I had no idea."

When I reach Diane's office, I sit down in front of Allen and say, "You were so upbeat yesterday. Have you had a crash?"

Allen wipes his eyes, sighs, and answers, "I don't know why. There was a fight upstairs, and I brought one of the boys down to the office. As I came down the stairs, something just hit me."

"I know. Just when you least expect it, memories come flooding back. When a dog runs in front of your car, you have no warning and may not even have time to hit your brakes. That's how I think of these unexpected flashbacks."

I'm glad I could give a moment of understanding to Allen; we don't talk every day, but we still have that unique connection between parents who have lost a child.

March 2009

Sometimes a teacher finds a way to connect with a difficult student when no one else can. Thomas was unmotivated, uncooperative, and on occasion defiant, but for some reason he listened to me. Through his journal writing and our conferences in the hall, I learned of his depression. I knew he lived near downtown Nashville in a housing project with a single mother. Thomas once told me he was sure he would not live to the age of 18; he fully expected to be killed in some violent act in his neighborhood.

Thomas needed a father figure and found one in Allen. If Allen planned a special movie or activity for his class either he sent word to me, asking permission for Thomas to join the class, or Thomas would ask me if he could go upstairs to Mr. B's class. I saw more interest and pleasure in Thomas' face on those occasions than any other time. I usually allowed him to visit, believing Allen provided Thomas support and encouragement.

June 2009

As this difficult school year ends, I look forward to the summer of rest. On the last day of in-service for teachers, the principal calls the faculty into the library at the end of the day for an unexpected meeting. Our school resource officer tells us that over the last few days he has been investigating a serious situation. He has uncovered a shocking discovery; Allen has been sexually abusing some of the boys after school in other locations. A wave of disbelief rolls over me, and then anger builds as the resource officer and principal give us the details. Teachers look at each other in disbelief. How could we all have missed this?

All this time I thought he was helping Thomas! I am shattered for Thomas and later learn he is the one who first revealed the abuse. But I am so angry at Allen! My mind is reeling with questions. I wait around in the library, hoping to learn more details. I share my anger with our resource officer who sympathizes with me. I think we all feel some guilt that we did not protect these boys, even though the abuse took place outside of school hours.

I wonder what part of Allen's story was a lie. Was the young man who died really Allen's son or just "one of his boys?" And now I am helpless to reach out to Thomas. The investigation continues but in the hands of the police and eventually makes the news. Allen has several outstanding warrants in Chattanooga, and he is eventually arrested there.

My head and heart have taken a beating this year. I finally lowered my defenses, took a chance at vulnerability and reached out to another wounded soul, only to learn of this betrayal of confidence and trust.

Before school ends Martha accepts a job at the nearby high school, and I realize I need to make some decisions. I do not want to stay at this school if she is gone, so I need to look for other options. I remember that a new middle school is opening just about a mile from my house in Madison. I quickly apply to the principal who happens to be a friend from church. Since an eighth-grade position is not available, I accept the sixth-grade, agreeing to teach them for a year and then move up to eighth grade the next year. I pack up my classroom, my home for nine years, and move my boxes out.

Summer

Most of the summer I prepare for a new school and a new curriculum; I gather the sixth-grade textbooks and plan units of instruction. As soon as I have a classroom assigned to me, I design learning centers and collect materials and furniture to put in place. Several days of summer workshops provide opportunities to meet the new faculty and plan for our first year together. My excitement for the challenges of a new year builds throughout the summer. I'm ready to teach sixth graders!

I follow my summer break pattern by picking up my journal and *The Ransomed Heart*. The following insights found a place in my journal:

> *The voice of God is never condemning, harsh, or accusing. His conviction makes us want to repent. Satan's accusation kills our heart.*[71]

> *Our life is a story — long and complicated. Imagine God walking beside me. He says, "Tell me your sorrows." My pride says, "I don't need therapy." We all need counseling. Jesus sent the Holy Spirit (the Comforter or Counselor) to be with us when He returned to heaven. He has come to stay.*[72]

This I Know Now:

I pray Thomas has been able to receive counseling and has found some peace in his life. When I watch the evening news, I look for faces of former students who might be involved in some crime.

Allen was eventually indicted in Chattanooga, but I can't find any information since 2009 regarding his case.

Despite all the depression and sadness involved in leaving friends, I eagerly accepted the change in grade as our new faculty bonded throughout the summer.

Now I Am Thankful for:

- Dr. Chambers' listening and alertness to needed changes in medication
- professionals at school who acted quickly once they knew we had a serious problem in our building

Your Turn:

- Don't worry about ANYTHING
- Pray about EVERYTHING, especially

_____

- Thank Him for all He has done.

Philippians 4:6-7

> *Then you will experience God's peace, which exceeds anything we can understand. His peace will guard your hearts and minds as you live in Christ Jesus. NLT*

Chapter 19
CHANGES

*If I turn my heart to God,
I open a door.*

School Year 2009-2010

Despite my many years of teaching, the group of sixth graders assigned to me is one of the most challenging of my career. My teaching partner and I share two groups of students by concentrating on our individual academic strengths. We eventually decide to self-contain to avoid the movement interruption of changing classes.

By the end of the school year, I gladly turn in my sixth-grade teacher's manuals and look forward to a new year with eighth graders. Several workshops are scheduled for the summer on literacy as well as a middle school conference in Gatlinburg.

June 16

Summer 2010

My quiet place arrives. I take time to slow down, take care of little things, and enjoy life. One major hiccup: weeding my iris bed results in a bad case of poison ivy; a steroid shot and pills for two weeks take care of it. Despite the past school year's struggles, I am determined to rest and rejuvenate this summer.

Early in June I develop an early morning schedule beginning at 6:00 or 6:30. I return to Ransomed Heart for meditation and study, use a yoga DVD for exercise, and inspect my garden before the heat of the day arrived.

Saying Good-bye

This summer is my time to care for the dying. Two aunts have cancer as well as my dear friend, Judy. I have avoided funerals as much as possible since 2002, but I feel a strong calling to minister to these loved ones.

Both aunts live a few miles from each other in north Georgia. Martha Ann, Mama's younger sister, lives with her daughter, Rene. She returned home from the hospital under the care of hospice. Brownie, my aunt on Daddy's side of the family, has a huge growth in her throat that interferes with swallowing. Radiation is the only treatment available for her. I haven't seen either of these dear aunts in several years, so I make plans to visit both.

July

Early in July I drive down to Georgia and stay with Rene and Martha Ann. We visit, share news of family, and reminisce. I spend more time listening to Rene; being her mother's full-time caregiver challenges her every day, but she gladly accepted the role. While at Rene's, I contact Brownie, and we arrange a meeting at a restaurant with two of her daughters. Brownie suffers trying to eat, but we still laugh and joke. I love connecting with these cousins I haven't seen in years and watching their interactions with each other. After my visit, I stay connected to my cousins through email.

When Aunt Martha Ann dies later in the summer, her funeral is in Tompkinsville, Kentucky. I drive up and meet her three children. We have a cousin reunion in Aunt Mayme's motel room, reconnecting after years of not seeing each other. The oldest of the three sisters, Mayme is the matriarch of us all – the last of her generation.

Aunt Brownie dies a few months later. At last her pain ends.

Monday, July 28

Some friendships can begin immediately upon meeting, have lapses in time, and pick up as if there had never been an interruption. My friend Judy and I had that kind of friendship; we met in the late 70's when we worked at the same special school. After a year she went to Vanderbilt to supervise student teachers; I learned so much from Judy about teaching language and sign language. She even gave me a baby shower before Jennifer's birth. Over the 15 years I taught middle school students with disabilities she assigned many practicum students and student teachers to my classroom. Even though we did not see each other for long periods of time, we could always resume our friendship as though no time had passed.

Judy's cancer has spread, and tumors continue to grow in her stomach; the doctor does not recommend more chemo. She is confined to a hospital bed in her front room. Even though she seems to be ready for hospice, I'm not sure her family is ready.

When I call Judy this morning, she sounds like an old woman barely able to speak, but she wants me to come about 1:00. I am surprised to see how thin she is – it is most apparent in her face. She tells me she might nod off and promises to let me know when she gets tired. Despite her best efforts, she struggles to stay awake. She tries to put her thoughts together but keeps repeating herself. My heart fills with sadness; Judy had one of the sharpest minds of anyone I have ever known.

Judy lays quietly with her eyes closed, so I pick up a book to read. She opens her eyes and says, "Tell me about school." Judy can always inspire me with some new creative idea, no matter what age or subject I am teaching. I describe the adventure expeditions I used with my sixth graders. Her brain immediately engages; an idea jumps out. It doesn't surprise me that she uses artist's materials to teach a lesson. I learned basket weaving, flower arranging, and book-making from Judy. "After students create a model from clay, tell them to smash it, illustrating that you can always remold yourself," she says. What a great activity for eighth graders at the beginning of the year, or after the first report card!

"I have some of the best books on writing by Fletcher. They are in my office." She visualizes them on the shelf of a room full of bookcases and tells me exactly where to find them. I go to her office, walk in, and immediately locate them. It seems Judy needed a purpose to get her brain working, but her energy soon begins to fade. As I prepare to leave, her hospice nurse arrives.

I spend another morning with Judy later in the summer. She gives me detailed instructions in preparing some potatoes in chicken broth, and then we watch a movie on TV, *Julie and Julia*. Whenever I see a clip of that movie, I think of the afternoon I spent with Judy. She loved to plan meals, share recipes, and cook for a crowd.

I am so glad I could make time for those visits with Judy. She dies in the fall; Emalie and I go to the memorial services. As their final days neared the time this summer allowed me opportunities to say goodbye and perhaps leave them with a little joy. When their pain finally ended, I felt sorrow but not inconsolable despair. Their readiness for death and our time together helped me let go without regrets.

Spiritual Path of Summer 2010

All summer I faithfully make time for quiet moments. I use *Ransomed* and fill a journal with notes as I dig into his writings on broken hearts.

Eldredge addresses my constant mantra in my journey of grief: guarding my heart. This passage in Proverbs 4:20-23 contains wise advice:

> *My child, pay attention to what I say.*
> *Listen carefully to my words.*
> *Don't lose sight of them.*
> *Let them penetrate deep into your heart,*
> *For they bring life to those who find them*
> *and healing to their whole body.*
> *Guard your heart above all else,*
> *for it determines the course of your life. NIV*

All this time of remembering to guard my heart, I didn't read the rest of the verse. The heart determines the course of my life! Eldredge calls the heart a treasure because everything else depends on it.[73]

I write this in my journal:

> *Guard your heart – this is what I tell people, that I guard*
> *my heart very carefully. I don't keep it open so that pain*

*and grief can surprise me. Of course, I can't always stop
those unexpected moments, and I need to be ready for them,
but I also can keep some feelings at arm's length.*

As I consider these references and entries on the heart, I reflect on the possibility of developing a study for a Bible class on broken hearts.

Another important reading in *Ransomed,* entitled "The Source of All Our Healing and All Our Strength," reminds me of some important truths:

- The only true home for my heart is abiding in God's love
- I must let my heart come home to God
- If I turn my heart to God, I open a door
- A deep intimate union with God can heal my broken heart[74]

School Beginnings, August 2010

I welcome my first class of eighth graders at my new school. First days are always just a half day (for several good reasons.) As the last buses pulled out of the drive, I search out my principal and tell her I have found my place again. I belong with eighth graders!

Our school faces many hurdles this fall, one of which is a new building. Our building is a remodel of a high school; on the first day of school painters are still painting, and electricians and plumbers can be found throughout the building. Everything is new to our students: lockers, restrooms, gym, dressing rooms, lunchroom, and these long hallways leading to various wings of the building. I am now becoming aware that the little school of fifth, sixth, and seventh-graders from where we taught last year is no more! At our new building, student enrollment is doubled as well as faculty and staff. New custodial and lunchroom staff mean new faces everywhere.

Beginning school in the fall is always stressful, and our new building, new staff, new students compound the stress. We are overwhelmed but don't figure out why until at least a month later. My eighth-graders are not just our last year's seventh graders; they include many students from other schools. From Day One, establishing routines, implementing a discipline plan, and procedures are essential for optimum learning; however, in several of my classes a battle of wills continues until the October fall break.

Stress is my companion every day. My health reacts; I have a racking cough that leaves my voice hoarse for weeks. A diagnosis of asthma surprises me! At the age of sixty-three I suffer from the same illness youngest brother Paul had as a child and oldest brother Steve continues to battle as an adult. This stress continues to build. Arthritis in my right knee makes walking painful and sometimes causes my knee to lock up. One day I have a complete meltdown in the office – just cannot stop crying. My principal gives me some excellent advice, "You have options."

October

When fall break arrives in October, I do some serious soul-searching. When I turned sixty I never set a specific date for retirement; my plan has always been to teach as long as it is fun. This is no longer fun! I talk to personnel at the school board about retirement and my financial options.

Larry continues to encourage me to retire; he knows I have reached my limit. I make the decision to retire and tell my principal when we return to school. I let her know my goal is to make it to the end of the semester in December.

Prayer About My Next Stage in Life.

Holy Father, Giver of life and grace,

I seek your blessings on this decision to retire from teaching. All the signs point to change – my health (allergies, knee pain, depression), my passion for teaching in difficult places, our finances, and a new challenge.

I have a part-time job waiting for me with an online university teaching the Bible.

Father, you know I have always felt my teaching was my mission. I believe I am called to teach and serve and mold the lives of the poor and unlovable. Now I see another place to serve – students around the world who want to learn the Bible.

Guide me through the next nine weeks as I pull my teaching tent down. Watch over me and give me good health to do what needs to be done.

Show me ways to draw closer to You in this new path. You know my heart has not been with you as it should have been.

Give me the wisdom I need in the next few months.

Thank you for all these blessings that have come my way

In your Son's precious name,

Amen

December

I make it to the end of the semester, barely. When I tell my classes of my decision, one of the girls comes to me and says, "Diamond is crying because she thinks you are retiring because of her!" Who knows what goes on in the minds of students? I begin a PowerPoint slide listing my reasons for retiring. I just kept adding more reasons as the day went on --- silliness, students who interrupt learning. The list grows to fifteen reasons!

This I Know Now:

I have never regretted retiring at the time I did. I felt the same way when I left Special Education and moved to general education. It was time to change. I don't miss teaching middle school students, although I do miss the camaraderie of a teaching team.

I have a recurring dream that I'm teaching again and trying to retire, but I keep saying I need to work one more day or one more week or even another year. The dream ends when I tell another teacher or an administrator that I am done. No more school teaching!

Thirty-three years is a long time to teach! I still have this dream after ten years of retirement.

The summer of visiting with dying family and Judy healed the wound that funerals had opened. A few years later I attended Mayme's funeral with no difficulty.

Now I Am Thankful for:

- retirement freedom and peace
- teaching in new ways – tutoring elementary children and teaching adult Bible classes
- the many opportunities I received to learn new strategies, serve in leadership capacities, and team with excellent teachers to create a stimulating and creative learning environment.

Your Turn:

- Don't worry about ANYTHING
- Pray about EVERYTHING
- Tell God what I NEED, not what I want

_____

- THANK Him for all He has done.

Philippians 4:6-7

> *Then you will experience God's peace, which exceeds anything we can understand. His peace will guard your hearts and minds as you live in Christ Jesus. NLT*

Chapter 20

VISION

You don't put a life on a shelf and forget it.

January 2011

I begin my new job early in January; I enjoy the challenge of learning new skills and meeting students in far-off countries with a burning desire to understand God's word. Part of my responsibility includes developing the plan for accreditation for the institution. This job provides a new environment, new co-workers, and a new culture for work. A good change from teaching middle school.

April

Working two and a half days a week provides me time for quiet meditation. I pick up *The Ransomed Heart* and take notes; I've completed about half of the book. In Reading #186 Eldredge considers a question I seldom voice but hold in a secret pocket of my heart, "God, why did you let this happen?" I know God could have protected Jennifer, and it just rolls through my mind. The writer says the real question we are asking, "Do you really care for me, God?"[75]

July

Nila asked me to teach her Sunday Ladies Bible Class for the month of July. For the first time, I look through my journals to organize lessons on this journey of grief I've been traveling. I use the metaphor of broken hearts, create PowerPoint slides and handouts for the four lessons.

This class of prayer warriors supply me with encouragement throughout the series; Nila's blessing gives me the courage to take this step in sharing my story.

Lesson One presents the main idea that we all have broken hearts. I pull together several Scriptures including Isaiah 61:1-3 (also in Luke 4) where we find a list of the Messiah's mission. This one phrase is my theme song – "He came to bind up the brokenhearted".

In Lesson Two, I focus on things that helped me during my hardest days of grief as well as those that did not help. Psalm 42, our trip to Starr Mountain, and my experiences at Trevecca. I also provide specific songs and a list of the books I continue to turn to for comfort and understanding. I read from some of my journals, producing a few tears to my listeners. I thank God I could deliver these lessons without drowning in painful emotions. The third lesson provides specific ways to comfort others who mourn. I explain the stages of grief as related in Walter Wangerin, Jr.'s book *Mourning into Dancing*.

August 2011

Journal notes from *The Ransomed Heart*

I discover a truth expressed in a way I have not considered:

> *"We all know the dilemma of desire, how awful it feels*
> *to open our hearts to joy, only to have grief come in.*
> *They go together."*[76]

The problem is we don't know what to do with this dilemma. I experience a broken heart over and over throughout my journey.

I am reminded of C.S. Lewis' words: *"To love at all is to be vulnerable."* The complete quote follows.

> *To love at all is to be vulnerable. Love anything and your*
> *heart will be wrung and possibly broken. If you want to*
> *make sure of keeping it intact you must give it to no one,*
> *not even an animal. Wrap it carefully round with hobbies*

*and little luxuries; avoid all entanglements. Lock it up safe
in the casket or coffin of your selfishness. But in that casket,
safe, dark, motionless, airless, it will change. It will not be
broken; it will become unbreakable, impenetrable, irre-
deemable. . .*[77]

November 23, 2011

One week after Jennifer's birthday, I receive a phone call from Courtney early in the morning from her hospital bed. She just gave birth to a little girl and wants me to know they named her Grace Jennifer. I am thrilled for her and touched; Jennifer and Courtney were so close while they were roommates at Tech.

January 2012

I resign from my job at the nonprofit university due to conflicts over poli-cies. After a few days of decompressing, my thoughts turn to a writing project nudging my conscience.

February 2012

A Writing Project

This prayer in my journal asks for God's blessings.

*I give to You, Father and Friend, this project to write
Jennifer's story. It was so clear to me last night, but now I
hesitate. Do I have enough of her journals?*

*I ask You to bless my efforts — my thinking and organizing.
Help me find the words to share a life. I have plenty for
the ending of the book, but is there enough for the middle?
Maybe I should reach out to her friends.*

*Ultimately, I put it in Your hands. You are the Holy One.
You're the One, You're the only One.*

Gathering Resources

During February I contact Courtney about tapping into her memories as well as their closest friends at Tech. I also ask her for Josh's email. Right after Jennifer died I gave away as many of her things as I could. I remember giving Josh some of her books, but my memory is not clear on the specifics. I hope he has some of her journals. I have all her childhood diaries and scrapbooks, and some of her high school journals.

I also contact Lajuana about the presentation she made back in 1999 for the high school girls in the area. I want to reconstruct the influences in Jennifer's life during her teen years as well as college years.

During a visit to West Tennessee, David and I discuss writing memoirs and my idea of writing a book from Jennifer's perspective. He suggests that I write this book in Jennifer's voice, revealing her death at the end of the book rather than the beginning. Since he is writing a fiction book, I am grateful for any advice he can give me.

I send Josh an email about my writing project; he lives in the county south of us with his wife and preschool daughter. I ask him if he still has any of Jennifer's things. "You may have just stuck them on a shelf and not even re-member where they are – which is okay. But I would love to see them."

He writes back the sweetest line, "You don't put a life on a shelf and forget it." We talk on the phone and set up a time to get together at his house.

Forming a Plan

I sort through all of Jennifer's journals, papers, and memorabilia from ele-mentary and high school, typing anything that I think I might use. I organize everything in a notebook and develop chapter titles using lines from songs from the movie, *Annie*. My working titles are *Hang On 'til Tomorrow* or *The Sun will Come Out Tomorrow*. She and Brooke played the soundtrack from *Annie* over and over, singing and acting out their favorite songs. The songs meander in and out of their lives like their own personal soundtrack. When Jennifer and Josh were on the top of Starr Mountain, she sang "The Sun Will Come Out" for him for the first time. And minutes later she ran down the trail, lost her balance and fell to her death.

I rediscover Jennifer's writing in a college autobiography, her high school frustrations and soul-searching journals, as well as childhood notebooks full of lists and notes to best friend, Brooke.

Josh

Josh invites me to have lunch at his house to pick up Jennifer's memorabilia. Josh, Lori, and I sit on their deck in the sunshine to eat lunch watching their daughter entertain us. After we eat, Josh and Lori bring in a blue trunk. Tangled emotions punch me in the stomach. I had forgotten about her trunk, the trunk that traveled to camp every summer and then three years to Tennessee Tech. It is plastered with pictures from camp, mission trips, high school, and college friends. How could I have forgotten this trunk?

When Josh opens it, he slowly pulled out notebooks and books. Then he says, "Will I ever get this back?"

I answer, "Of course! I only want it to help me write this book."

We sort through things I can use: a memory jar she gave him one Christmas when she had no money for gifts, her Bible, workbooks, and folders full of writing. It holds a wealth of memories for both of us – a real-life treasure chest.

After loading the trunk in my car, I head north to Madison. Larry and I leave the trunk in the living room for several days while we immerse ourselves reading moments of Jennifer's life as viewed through her eyes.

February 23

Chambers' words jump off the page sometimes, and this reading is one of them. "Sometimes God puts us through the experience and discipline of darkness to teach us to hear and obey Him. How slow I have been to listen and understand what God has been telling me! And yet God has been saying it for days and even weeks."[78]

February 27

When I dig into these memories of Jennifer, sorrow begins to overwhelm me. I need to trust in my Savior and ask for strength.

Holy God,

I have failed to seek your comfort with these feelings of sadness. You know this pain, and You can pull me through. Writing this book stirs my emotions; reaching out to Courtney and Josh has been emotional. As a result, I've been selfish, thinking of what I need to do and leaving Larry out in the process.

Remind me Lord to include him in this process. Help me to be more open to his needs.

Bless my efforts to volunteer at Madison Middle School tomorrow. I pray it will support Katie and reach students. I ask that you care for the teachers and staff, give them comfort, healing, courage, and support . . .

March 2

Retreat at Woodmont

Lark encourages our Girlfriend Group to attend the Woodmont Women's Retreat in March. All but Carrie can make it. Friday's weather forecast changes the retreat plans since the retreat location required traveling east into predicted tornadoes. Organizers canceled the Friday night plans; instead, we meet at the church building Saturday morning for a day of activities.

The theme of the retreat is based on Ann Voskamp's book *One Thousand Gifts*. I purchase my book early and read just a little of the introduction. The first lines in the book grab my attention:

> *Really, when you bury a child . . . you murmur the question soundlessly. No one hears. "Can there be a good God?"*
>
> *Where is God, <u>really?</u> How can He be good when babies die, . . .?*[79]

My first thoughts: I know these questions. I grab a highlighter and begin marking.

Saturday Morning

Round tables beautifully decorated for spring fill the meeting room. At the registration table I choose one of the empty journals in a basket and find a seat waiting for me at Lark's table. The rest of our group settle in at the table, but Joan keeps working on retreat details as well as the meal for later in the day.

Ann Voskamp's ideas of counting our gifts unfold through the morning as young women share stories of their difficult paths. We stop periodically to count gifts and write in our journals. Bare tree branches are placed around the room, waiting for us to write down a blessing and tie it to the tree.

During a break, Lark presents each of us a copy of her newest favorite book, *Jesus Calling* by Sarah Young. She also has another tool that caught my attention - a prayer cross made of clay and shaped to hold in the hand.

Both Voskamp's and Young's books are inviting me in; I can't wait to dig into each one.

Late in the morning, several people receive text messages about a horrible car accident involving several young men from the Woodmont church family. Two carloads of students from Harding University were traveling to Texas for Spring Break. The first vehicle was rear-ended; when Ty gets out of his truck to check on the other car, another car rear-ends his truck, severely injuring Ty.

We learn bits and pieces of the story during the day, finally hearing that Ty is airlifted to a nearby hospital. Prayers are breathed for all the students, but especially Ty; his injuries are critical, and his chances of survival are slim.

The families of these college students are close to many of the women at the retreat. The lessons of the day suddenly hit each one of us; life can change in an instant. Plans for the afternoon activities change; we gather in a large circle to worship. Songs of praise and petitions of mercy are lifted for healing and safety. I speak about the importance of a circle of friends in these moments. I tell stories of how our Girlfriend Circle supported me through the many ups and downs of my journey following Jennifer's untimely death.

As we clean up at the end of the day Joan and I talk about the blessing of sharing with one another today during such a difficult time. God's timing, His movement through our lives continues to amaze and surprise us. Despite the emotional events of the day, I keep my own feelings locked away.

I leave with new tools I can't wait to use.

This I Know Now:

Teaching the Bible Class on Broken Hearts marked a significant point of transition in my grief. I studied each week, prepared, and delivered lessons with ease.

Sharing advice at the retreat during an intensely emotional time seemed as natural for me as an opportunity before Jennifer's death. I didn't need time to prepare my thoughts or my heart.

The young man so seriously injured in the accident did not survive; the whole church family suffered a great loss. I did not know Ty's family, but I wrote a card to his mom offering support, encouragement, and sympathy.

Now I Am Thankful for:

- Lark's invitation to the retreat and the time we had together in the Girlfriend Circle
- Ann Voskamp's book, _One Thousand Gifts_, opening a door for me
- Sarah Young's book, _Jesus Calling_, a favorite I continue to use today.

Your Turn:

- Don't worry about ANYTHING
- Pray about EVERYTHING
- Tell God what I NEED
- THANK Him for all He has done.

- In my circumstance today, I may not be able to see His gifts and blessings, but I can find at least three blessings today.

_____

_____
_____

_____

Philippians 4:6-7

Then you will experience God's peace, which exceeds anything we can understand. His peace will guard your hearts and minds as you live in Christ Jesus. NLT

Chapter 21
PERSPECTIVE

*Changing our perspective
can reveal an answer
we did not even know was available.*

March 2012

On the day of the Women's Retreat, I begin counting gifts. I faithfully write in a journal of thanks each day; Ann's suggestion is to write three gifts a day, thus reaching 1000 within a year. When I begin writing, I don't stick with three a day; I just write as many as I can.

A new gift of joy enters our lives in early March – Courtney's two-year-old Grace comes to our house every other Friday. This helps Courtney with daycare problems, and we are delighted to welcome Grace Jennifer into our lives.

Gifts Counted:

- Larry and Grace laughing, playing, enjoying each other
- Grace snuggled in my lap as we rocked and watched Dora, the Explorer
- Such an easy day with this two-year-old
- Larry's whole morning devoted to being with Grace

- Courtney's love for Jennifer when I showed her the blue trunk covered with pictures of Jennifer. Many of the pictures included Courtney.

Journaling

I begin a daily practice of reading the Scriptures from *Jesus Calling* and then journaling the key points for the daily reading.

> God says, "I can fit everything into a pattern of good – only to the extent that I trust Him. Every problem can teach me something, transforming me. The best way to befriend problems is to THANK Him for them. He will not necessarily remove them, but His wisdom is to bring good out of every one of them.[80] This thanking God now comes to me from two sources, Ann's book and <u>Jesus Calling</u>. Must be important!

> Prayer: Lord, I pray to gain Your perspective on my life as You shine Peace into my heart and mind.

On March 15 I begin a careful slow reading of *One Thousand Gifts*. I highlight and keep notes of important observations. Ann's style of writing and language work new thoughts into my heart. Her questions to God and her personal journey through years of grief, depression, and everyday living speak directly to me. Her question echoes the question lying just beneath the surface throughout my journey: *"How do I full live when life is full of hurt?"*[81]

March 18

Reflection from Chapter 3

> I pray that God who gives Hope will fill you with much Joy and Peace while you Trust in Him. Then your Hope will overflow by the power of the Holy Spirit." Romans 15:13 NIV

Using my new perspective, I'm learning from Voskamp's book this verse conveys the message that my hands <u>must be</u> <u>open</u> to receive joy and peace. God will not drop a bucket of joy or peace in my hands. I probably won't even recognize it because joy comes in the moments of a gift. Recognizing a gift can bring peace.

> *Prayer: God, I open my hands to every "Thank You", for every moment we had with Jennifer, for every good gift You put in her life – including her insight to her own spiritual growth. I trust You to make me strong as I write her story. I cannot do it alone, and I cannot see my way through this. Her words in her journal are sinking into my bones – now they need a narrative around them.*

Gifts Counted:

- Deeper understanding of joy, peace, and the connection to gratitude
- God's strength when I am weak
- This list is God's list that opens my soul to receive His gift of joy
- energy to write, shop, pick up prescriptions, iron Larry's clothes
- Larry's recovery from flu
- energy to knit a scarf for Brenda
- more pieces coming together of Jennifer's life
- Dollar Tree toys for Grace
- redbud trees in bloom

April 5

Reflection from Chapter 5

I find Chapter 5 the hardest chapter of Voskamp's book to summarize. She asks the hard questions about the suffering we experience and then reconciling it with a gracious all-powerful God. Sometimes her answers are just more questions! Here are some of those questions:

"Are My ways your ways?" Isaiah 55:8 God reminds us that His thoughts are not our thoughts and His ways are not our ways.

"Who deserves <u>any</u> grace?"[82]

"Should we accept good from God, and not trouble?" Job 2:10 *NIV*

April 12

Tomorrow – ten years ago Jennifer died. How can it be?

Lessons I'm learning from Ann Voskamp:

> *Looking is the love. Looking is the evidence of the believing."*[83] *Complaints of Manna from Numbers 21 - God sent snakes. Ingratitude makes the poison course through their bodies. The remedy was to <u>look</u>, look at the bronze snake God told Moses to make.*

> *How we behold, determines if we hold joy…How we look, determines how we live …<u>if</u> we live.*[84]

> *…faith is always a way of <u>seeing</u>, a seeking for God in everything.*[85]

April 13

With no plans for honoring Jennifer on the tenth anniversary of her death or distracting myself, I think of Courtney's stepmother, Lisa, keeping vigil in the Vanderbilt burn ward for her daughter. I email Courtney to see if I could help in some way.

At 9:00 A.M. Lark calls to see if I have plans for the day. She wonders if we can get together for dinner. I'm always ready to meet a few of the Girlfriends.

I decide to make Joy in a Box for Lisa. Just this month Ann V.'s blog has photos and clipart for making a box to give someone. I call Lisa and make a plan to meet her at the hospital at 4:00. I'll meet Lark and Kathy at a pizza place (with gluten-free crusts) nearby.

I race around doing errands: buy gas, stop at Dollar Tree, Dollar Store, Christian Book Store, Hobby Lobby gathering materials for a box. I rush home to assemble the box and get to Vandy on time. Lisa loves the box; I include a journal, a copy of Ann's book, little things to ease the long waits between visits with her critically injured daughter.

Kathy and Lark are already at the restaurant when I arrive; we stay until after 10:00 P.M. We never run out of conversation. They want to know about my progress on the book. I described Jennifer's journals and her amazing insights into her own spiritual journey.

Truly a day of celebration. This is how I like to spend the anniversary of Jennifer's death, serving others, seeing old friends who remember her.

Reflections from Chapter 6

I ponder a repeating theme in the book, how to see grace in the ugly of this life. Ann calls this hard "eucharisteo." One evening she leaves dinner unserved, children clamoring around her, runs outside to chase the harvest moon. *"Praying with eyes wide open is the only way to pray without ceasing."*[86] I have the urge to write these words on a huge banner that I must touch every day.

April 16

Prayer

> *Help me Lord to see grace in the ugly. I confess I was*
> *unable to do that in my last two years of teaching. My*
> *students had ugly things in their lives, and it could show up*
> *as anger, indifference, defiance or rudeness. It reminds me*
> *of a statement I used in my dissertation: "They are bleeding*
> *inside."*

April 19 - Gifts Counted:

- a day with Grace!

- sunshine, wind, and the park with Grace and Larry
- squealing all the way down the big slide through the tube
- she runs around to the ladder, "You stay here," she says.
- Eating her lunch as she sits in a bright pink Dora chair
- naps for EVERYONE

May

I finish Ann's book and sign up to follow her blog for more inspiring words.

Since the retreat in March, I have been faithful to spend each morning with Scripture, prayer, journal, and counting gifts journal. After two and a half months I have 795 gifts listed. I find myself writing gifts before I sleep at night as well as in the morning. Ann's example motivates me to look for the smallest joy in counting. I appreciate the spring mornings and the entertaining mockingbirds who nest in my ferns and bushes.

June

Nila asks me to teach her Bible class again in July. Ann's book continues to impact my thinking, so I decide to try to teach her book in five weeks! My mind immediately jumps to creating some way to highlight important phrases. I settle on banners for the classroom; I shop at JoAnn's and purchase fabric needed. The next weeks are filled by making banners and creating lessons with PowerPoint.

The highlight of the month for me is the opportunity to hear Ann Voskamp in person at a local church. Lark and I attend and drink up her message. This large gathering of women fills the auditorium with songs of praise and worship!

Last July I told my story of grief in the Bible class, but until I started counting gifts I didn't feel like I had much to offer others. This new perspective has slowly seeped into my being, and I do feel joy again. It's not magic, and it did not happen all at once. Grief is a process.

"When I give thanks for the microscopic, I make a place for God to grow within me."[87]

Recognizing a gift can bring peace. When you focus on how you are blessed, it changes your perspective.

August

Sharing the Story

I begin writing a blog to share the journey of grief over Jennifer's death and call it "countingjoyblog". I set a goal of writing three times a week, using Friday's post for Heart Lessons. Writing these posts solidify my path for writing a book. After planning a book about Jennifer, I slowly came to a realization: I can't write Jennifer's story without writing my story first. My memories keep getting in the way as I think about her story. I must lay out all my memories and heartaches before I write her story.

October

Another step in the journey of sharing this story takes place at the Woodmont church. I speak at a luncheon about the lessons I've learned practicing giving thanks each day. Joan planned the luncheon and introduces me. Speaking, even about grief, now is as natural as walking for me. After visiting with friends, I stop at Scarritt Bennett Center near Vanderbilt's campus to walk the labyrinth. Fall leaves crunch as I step slowly on the winding path and contemplate the blessings and gifts in my life, despite my long walk ten years in the valley of grief.

December

Blog entry

My life is enriched and blessed by the spiritual depth of Ann Voskamp's blog, the group of writers at "(in)courage" and "Women of Faith."

The blessings I have received since launching my blog come from readers who tell me the words have helped them. I believe the words come from God's blessings, but their comments are gifts to me. Sometimes I hesitate to dig into those memories and tell the story of my grief, but I remember that each reader is likely in a different place in their own grief, and my story might be helpful. The blog has been a safe and supportive place to write about my journey each

Friday in posts under the heading of Heart Lessons. The thing about grievers is this - just because it has been five years or five months since a death, the recovery or healing is still in process.

This I Know Now:

- Ann Voskamp's books impacted my life so much that I continue to give away her gift books. I've read *One Thousand Gifts* at least three times.
- Naming the gifts provided a structure that continues to guide me. My journals filled with daily lists begin in 2012 and continue today.
- I learned from Kate Motaung that grief is not a process to graduate from. It is a cyclical journey.
- Writing the blog provided more healing as well as experience in writing three times a week.

Now I Am Thankful for:

- healing enough to share my experiences by speaking and writing
- Grace in our lives for three years, watching her grow and change!
- lifting of depression this year

Your Turn:

- Don't worry about ANYTHING, even

- Pray about EVERYTHING

- Tell God what I need
- Thank Him for all He has done.

Philippians 4:6-7

> *Then you will experience God's peace, which exceeds any-thing we can understand. His peace will guard your hearts and minds as you live in Christ Jesus. NLT*

Epilogue
THIS I KNOW IN 2018

*When you are grieving, you may feel as if
sorrow will accompany you for the rest of your days.*[88]

The Story I Was Told

Being a wife and mother fulfilled God's purpose for my life.

The Story I Told Myself

I wanted and planned to be a wife and mother. Teaching school would be the best occupation for me because I would have afternoons and summers off to be with my children.

The Story Life Told Me

I did not have children for the first ten years of marriage. I finally gave that desire and brokenness to God, praying His will be done.

When I became pregnant I almost lost this long-desired baby. During the first trimester, I was bedridden until the risk was gone. I prayed to God for this baby to live but also for His will to be done.

Jennifer was a gift from God from her first breath. The second gift was that I was able to stay home with her for much of her first three years. When she was a few months old, we went to a Mother's Day Out program three days a week. I taught the two-year-old class. When she was almost two we went to a private church school, and I taught kindergarten half a day while she stayed in a class for her age.

As she grew I watched her struggle with shyness, fears, lack of self-confidence in elementary school. Then she began to bloom with confidence in color guard, challenge herself in high school to change her image, run track, go on mission trips to Jamaica, and climb mountains.

When she died, she loved a man who loved God as much as she did and knew where she wanted to serve God.

Her death shattered my bubble of contentment while my grief changed my view of God, sending me on a search for my purpose. The journey of grief has lasted sixteen years, and I expect it to continue until I die.

Uninvited Guest

November 2015, Journal Entry

You would think that I would know when Depression was coming - or that I would recognize it right away. While buying groceries in the late afternoon, I noticed my energy had disappeared. Larry helped me bring in the groceries. After I put them away, I vegetated, tired, not caring about supper, not making any plans.

I pulled out some leftover corn chowder for me and made Larry grilled cheese and bacon sandwiches with his help. By 7:00 PM I knew I was depressed.

When I went to bed, I did some reflection and remembered my neglect of keeping a daily Thanks Journal and prayer time. I started listing blessings in my journal while sitting in bed. My list was longer than usual because it had been several days since I had written. And then the most amazing thing happened! I've been through a few episodes of depression in the last thirteen years, but this had never happened: the weight lifted, the knot disappeared. I no longer felt the physical symptoms of my Depression.

Reeve Lindbergh says that sadness became a member of her family after the death of her son. Horror faded but this sadness was left behind. (*No More Words*). My depression visits me without an invitation; it drops in uninvited when I'm not expecting it. I can't say I have any affection for it as Lindbergh does. It's more like a difficult relative whose presence makes everyone uncomfortable.

As I closed my journal I asked God to keep depression away the next day. When I awoke? No depression; the uninvited left without a word and has not revisited. Good riddance, I say.

I never want the practice of writing down my gifts to seem trite or magical, but something happens to my soul when I look for the blessings of each day, even in the most difficult of situations.

Healing

What does time do for a broken heart? What does time do for a journey of grief?

This is what I've learned about time: The rawness of pain fades slowly. The passage of time does not diminish memories or missing Jennifer.

It took years for my heart to heal, but healing does not mean my heart returned to the same state as before April 13, 2002. Healing from grief is not a gradual improvement; it's two steps forward, then one step back. Or it's 20 steps back, and I'm once again immobile on the couch. It takes more than the passage of time to heal a heart.

Heart-healing does not heal like surgery or medication. My purpose in writing this book is to show mourners as well as those who want to assist the brokenhearted that the journey through hard times is not a smooth path. The road is rough, steep, dips into dark valleys, comes out into blue skies, and then hits some gullies. No two roads are the same; my healing will never look yours or my husband's or anyone else's. I'm still learning about healing.

My healing needed a network of supportive friends and family, research and locating helpful tools, the practice of quiet moments for Bible study, prayer and communion with the Father. Healing required me to learn and accept my limitations. Just when I thought I could move ahead, I was reminded that everything had changed. I am not the same person. Time helped the rawness of pain, but God had many lessons for me to learn in my journey of grief.

I never expected spiritual brokenness, but today my spiritual heart is mended. What called me back home? The anchor, the abiding place and comfort found only in the arms of my Father. He is my home. I found joy again through counting gifts, sharing my story, and teaching Bible classes. From the time I was sixteen I taught children's Bible classes while the only adults I taught were Bible class teachers who wanted some new ideas. I even wrote Sunday School curriculum for children. God surprised me with a different opportunity in retirement years; I'm teaching adult Bible classes! I'm digging into Scripture with online study tools and loving the challenge. The past two years of studying Psalms and Hebrews have enriched and increased my appreciation for God's Word. I spent one-year memorizing Romans 1, 8, and 12 following Ann Voskamp's challenge. The Word truly dwells in your heart when you spend time memorizing.

Psalm 40 continues to speak to my soul.

"He lifted me out of the slimy pit, out of the mud and mire.
He set my feet on a rock, gave me a firm place to stand.
He put a new song in my heart, a hymn of praise to our God."

Psalm 40:2-3 NIV

Help

In Anne Lamott's book *Stitches,* I found this compelling statement. *"The American way is to not need help, but to help. One of the hardest lessons I had to learn was that I was going to need a lot of help, and for a long time."*[89]

When Jennifer died, I had to relearn so many things; accepting help was the only thing I could do at first. When I stumbled through those first days and weeks of grief, I had to have help; my heart was broken, and my mind was in shock. Months and years went by before I could offer help to the grieving. The times I forgot my own pain resulted in disaster. My heart would ambush me and break open again with tears, sadness, even depression.

I continue to learn, to find ways to help others that work for me. Sometimes sending cards or cooking a meal allow me to help without an emotional connection, while on the other hand a phone call or a visit is possible.

It has taken me years to complete the writing of this book. Many days I had to stop because of depression. I pray God uses these words to heal the broken hearts of others.

Dear Father,

Show us when and how to help others, but also teach us how to just "be" with someone as they grieve, or weep, or lament.

Appendix 1:
SUGGESTIONS FOR HELPING

"Let me know if you need anything!"

How often I heard this statement after Jennifer died. No doubt, I have said it myself to others.

Although the offer is made with sincere intention to help, words alone do not help grievers. The newly brokenhearted don't always know what they need or feel free to ask, especially right after a death or burial. When the mourner needs you, you may not be available. This happened once with me. I called someone to ask for help, but she was not able to help me that day. I was devastated, just because I needed her for a specific task and could not gather my thoughts into a different plan of action.

The following list details needs that can be filled by others. Family members may take care of some items, but when you make a specific offer, the mourner has an opportunity to think about their own needs. For example, when Jim, a church member who brought food to our home the day after Jennifer's death, asked me if we needed anything else, I suddenly realized we needed to pick up Larry's brother and sister-in-law at the airport. We were overwhelmed with so many details; we were delighted someone else could make the trip to the airport.

When the funeral was over, shock took over my body and soul. I needed help but didn't know it.

Remembering how our church family provided so much compassion and support for us, I can't imagine how we could have managed without them. Friends, neighbors, co-workers, or other organizations may provide the same support if you are not part of a church family. I suggest that close friends take the lead in organizing some of these activities.

The Meal of Healing

In funeral traditions of the South, people bring food to the home of the mourners, to the funeral home for the family during visitation, or to the church building after the funeral. In the Jewish tradition, a meal will take place after the service at the cemetery. Whatever the tradition and customs in your community, providing food conveys the message that this is one thing the family does not have to worry about – preparing meals or even going out to eat meals.

During the First Days after a Death

Close friends and/or family members can assist with:

- Funeral arrangements
- Prayers, hugs, presence
- Writing obituary
- Writing funeral program
- Arranging pictures, memorabilia for visitation
- Assistance with extra flowers and plants after the funeral
- Organizing the food in the kitchen
- Keep a list of visitors and what they bring (food, flowers, gifts)
- Lawn care, pet care
- Answer the phone and/or the door

Others can assist with:

- Food at visitation (for family)
- Food supplies: plates, cups, ice, napkins
- Transportation for out of town family members

- Housing for out of town family
- Creating a slide presentation for the funeral

In the First Weeks after a Death

One or two close friends need to take the responsibility to check on specific needs. Visit the mourner and go through the list of possible needs. If the mourner is still in shock or just apathetic, gently ask if you can do some laundry or run errands. You don't want to be intrusive, but he/she may need a nudge to get out of the house for lunch, or perhaps you may notice some things that you can do. Not everyone will feel comfortable allowing others to do these tasks, but you won't know until you ask.

Using this list of possibilities may help the mourner think of other things you or others can do.

- Household: Laundry, cleaning, bathrooms, kitchen, floors, yard work, home maintenance, organization (paying bills, etc.)
- Errands: post office/mail, dry cleaner, pharmacy, deliveries, driving, rides to appointments
- Caregiving: pet and/or plant care, babysitting, children's homework help, outings
- Food: a regular schedule or occasional, freezer or crockpot meals, gift cards to restaurants
- Financial: funeral costs (GoFundMe set up/admin), gift cards (takeout, massage, manicure)
- Prayer: ongoing, specific times, praying together (prayer partner)
- Fellowship: lunch dates, exercise partner, shopping trips
- Moral Support: someone to listen without judgment, mental health day

First Months After a Death

- Set up a year-long prayer schedule

- This works well in a church or Bible class. Provide a sign-up sheet (see the example that follows) then ask one person (or more) to sign up for a specific date each month. Every month for a year someone will be praying every day for the mourner and their family. Send a letter to the family to let them know who is praying for them.

During the Next Year

- Don't forget this family or friend. It is so easy to become isolated during times of grief and heartache. It happens slowly, quietly, and may not even be obvious to the griever. Learn to "read" your friend and give him or her what is needed.
- Cards and prayers
- Especially one month from the date of death, send a card, make a phone call, pray, or post something on social media.

First Death/Divorce Anniversary

Close friends can plan some type of outing to acknowledge the day: lunch date or volunteer work in honor of the loved one. Acquaintances can send cards and messages of condolence.

Sitting Shiva

The following suggestions about Sitting Shiva may be unfamiliar to you but read through it and then consider trying it within your own community.

> *...what good people can do in the face of great sorrow.*
> *We help some time pass for those suffering. We sit with them*
> *in their hopeless pain and feel terrible with them, without*
> *trying to fix them with platitudes; doing this with them is*
> *just about the most gracious gift we have to offer. We give*
> *up what we think we should be doing, or think we need to*
> *get done, to keep them company.* —Anne Lamott[90]

In the Jewish faith, sitting Shiva means sitting with the griever for seven

(Shiva) days. The following suggestions modify some of the Jewish customs; the point is to provide a structured way to assist the mourner right after the funeral. Sometimes just sitting with a mourner is all that is needed; sometimes just having a person listen to stories about the deceased helps.

Suggestions for Approaching the Mourner and Offering Help

The day after the funeral a close friend should approach the mourner, preferably in person, and offer to arrange for someone to be at the home for specific times of the day – based on the preferences of the mourner. You can use this explanation:

> *I know these first days are going to be hard and you may want to be alone, but you also might want someone here to answer the phone, answer the door, or just be with you. We want to give you whatever assistance you need. If you need a sandwich, someone will be here to make it for you. If you want someone to pray with you or listen to your questions and lament, we can do that.*
>
> *I'll ask people you know to be here whenever you need them. If you are not sure about this, we can try it and then stop when you are ready. I'll be your contact person and arrange the schedule.*
>
> *The Jewish faith calls this sitting Shiva, meaning sitting with someone for seven days. You may not want someone that long, or you may not want anyone, but change your mind later.*
>
> *This is about what you need, and no one wants to be intrusive; we want to give you the support and comfort that helps you.*

I read about a widow who didn't want to see anyone after the death of her husband; her good friend stayed with her, taking in food, thanking people, but not allowing any visitors. She was the go-between the widow needed to give her time to mourn privately.

Everyone grieves in their own way, so don't be offended or hurt if the mourner turns you down. Making the offer is what counts. Remember how fragile life will seem after losing a loved one. Offering to help in times of crisis can be intimidating for those who have never done so. Perhaps you feel inadequate or fear you won't know what to say. Making the offer to do something is the first step. Learn to find a comfortable space with silence when you are with a mourner. Just being there, sitting and taking your cues from your friend can be the most supportive thing to do. Before you leave, ask if he or she would like you to pray.

Other situations of broken hearts need the same comfort and support: a single mother right after a divorce, families who suffer devastating fires or other disasters, loss of a job, diagnosis of cancer. The chronically ill or those taking chemo treatments need some of the same assistance. The list of suggestions can be adapted to meet each need. Another group of families needing attention are those with children who have disabilities. Their needs change constantly, depending on the age of the child and the severity of the disability.

Going with another friend can make this mission easier. Ask for God's guidance each step of the way. You will find a blessing in this work.

PRAYING EVERY DAY FOR A YEAR

Sign up for one day of the month and then mark your calendar for that same day every month for the next year reminding you to pray for the

_____ family

1._____   17._____
2._____   18._____
3._____   19._____
4._____   20._____
5._____   21._____
6._____   22._____
7._____   23._____
8._____   24._____
9._____   25._____
10._____   26._____
11._____   27._____
12._____   28._____
13._____   29._____
14._____   30._____
15._____   31._____
16._____

The family's address:

_____

Please send the family a note letting them know the day you are praying for them each month. It is not necessary to send a note every month but hearing from someone every day will be appreciated by those who are grieving.

Appendix 2:

A BUTTERFLY, ANY BUTTERFLY, WILL ALWAYS REMIND ME OF JENNIFER.

Two months before Jennifer's death, she led a high school girls' retreat using the theme of God's grace that changes us from our old self into a New Creature. She used a sweet book published many years ago: *Hope for the Flowers.*[91]

Just as a butterfly emerges from the cocoon into a completely new life, a new life of lightness and freedom emerges after the grace of God transforms us.

God's mercy should not feel heavy.

It is as light as a butterfly

but it covers everything.

Everything we do.

Everything we are.

Everything we were.

His grace is rich and is lavished on us.

In him we have redemption

through his blood,

the forgiveness of sins,

in accordance with the riches

of God's grace

that he lavished on us

with all wisdom and understanding.

Ephesians 1:7-8 NIV

I am thankful today for God's rich mercy and grace that he lavished on me. If you still carry a load of guilt because of a past you cannot forget, I pray you can lay that guilt at the cross and not pick it up again because you and I are covered!

APRIL 2014

Joy Martell Souder

No longer held together with fine thread,

the pieces of my broken heart were kept safe,

and finally put back in place,

one at a time,

held together by glue,

the glue of promises.

God's promises walked with me

through the dark valley of death.

He promised to be with me and watch over me,

even when I could not find Him.

Verse by verse, layer upon layer,

promises connected the pieces of

my broken heart,

made it stronger.

The pain has eased,

not gone and never forgotten.

My mended heart treasures

April's blooms on the saucer magnolia shrub

outside my kitchen window.

Planted by dear friends on April 2003,

reminding us of the joy

in Jennifer's life and

the impact of her life.

A PRAYER FOR MEDITATION

Joy Martell Souder

"Empty me, Lord, empty me.

Take away thoughts and images that distract me

Let them fall into a river that washes them out to the sea.

Empty my mind, my heart, my soul

So that You can fill me.

Open my eyes to your love, your gifts, your creation.

Illuminate the gifts that flow from your love

So that I am united with You in my love for You.

Joy will overflow my heart; I will be filled with Your Spirit."

Some of these words remind me of an old song, written by Clara Scott in 1895.

Chorus:

Silently now I wait for Thee,
Ready, my God, thy will to see:
Open my eyes, illumine me,
Savior divine!

Appendix 3:
BOOK RECOMMENDATIONS

These books provided me with inspiration, comfort, insight, and wisdom.

- *Have You Seen Marie?* Sandra Cisneros
- *Healing Through the Dark Emotions: The Wisdom of Grief, Fear, and Despair,*. Miriam Greenspan
- *Jesus Calling,* Sarah Young
- *Lament for a Son,* Nicholas Wolterstorff
- *Letters to Grief,* Kate Motaung.
  eBook found on her website: https://katemotaung.com/
- *Mourning into Dancing,* Walter J. Wangerin
- *My Utmost for His Highest,* Oswald Chambers
- *No More Words,* Reeve Lindbergh
- *One Thousand Gifts: A Dare to Live Fully Right Where You Are,* Ann Voskamp
- *Seven Sacred Pauses: Living Mindfully Through the Hours of the Day,* Macrina Wiederkehr
- *The Broken Way: A Daring Path into the Abundant Life,* Ann Voskamp

- *The Divine Hours: Prayers for Autumn and Wintertime,* Phyllis Tickle
- *The Ransomed Heart,* John Eldredge
- *The Sacred Way,* Tony Jones
- *The Song of the Seed: A Monastic Way of Tending the Soul,* Macrina Wiederkehr
- *Through a Season of Grief,* Bill Dunn and Kathy Leonard
- *Turning My Mourning into Dancing,* Henry Nouwen
- *When the Heart Waits,* Sue Monk Kidd
- *When There Are No More Words: Finding Your Way to Cope with Loss and Grief,* Charlie Walton
- *You'll Get Through This,* Max Lucado

Fiction writers who inspire and often include themes of redemption and grace in the face of tragedy:

- Susan May Warren
- Mary Alice Monroe
- Jan Karon
- Francine Rivers

Acknowledgments

My Encouragers

Nila's Sunday Morning Bible Class: you always supported me through your prayers, love, and encouragement. Thank you.

My Readers

Belinda, Anne, and Judy: Your skills, insight, and honesty made this a better book.

My Co-teacher and Friend

Carlene: You gave me time to complete this book, always encouraging and supporting me.

My Support Team at Donelson Middle School

Martha, Michelle, Linda, Matt, Belinda, Robbie, Diane, Carol, Damon, Rob: You stood with me at the casket, covered my classes, took care of problems I did not even see, allowed me to grieve in my own way. What a gift!

Courtney, Josh, and Lora Thank you for allowing me to share parts of your story.

Best Friend, Encourager, Motivator, Partner in Crime Scenes (leaving this for a different book!), Fearless Defender

Emalie: We've walked with each other through divorce, weddings, court, college graduations, and funerals. Twenty-six years: how rich, how deep, how wide is this friendship!

My Writing Mentor, Counselor, and Brother: David.

You never wavered in your belief that I could write this story. You gave me the first edits that motivated me to improve the writing, and then you guided me through each step of the publishing process. Your help was invaluable! Thank you.

Gail Cleare

Thank you for walking with me through selecting and creating the cover and holding my hand through the formatting of an ebook and much more.

Family

Steve, David, and Paul, their wives and children; Gary, Ruthann, children, and grandchildren, extended families: Thank you for always being there in too many ways to count.

Larry

My partner and husband for almost fifty years: "Thanks" cannot express my gratitude for the countless ways you made this book possible, especially all the times I couldn't stop to cook supper or get to the grocery store. We survived a horrible trauma together and by God's grace are able to serve Him in our own unique ways.

Endnotes

1. Motaung, Kate. *Letters to Grief.* (Kate Motaung, 2014).

2. https://en.wikipedia.org/wiki/Broken_heart#cite_note-4

3. https://bpdfamily.com/content/broken-heart-can-hurt-you

4. https://www.mayoclinic.org/diseases-conditions/broken-heart-syndrome/symptoms-causes/syc-20354617

5. Zisook, S; Shuchter, SR (October 1991). "Depression through the first year after the death of a spouse". *American Journal of Psychiatry.* **148 (10): 1346–52**. doi:10.1176/ajp.148.10.1346

6. van der Kolk, Bessel A; McFarlane, Alexander C; Weisæth, Lars (1996). *Traumatic Stress: The Effects of Overwhelming Experience on Mind, Body, and Society*. New York: Guilford Press. ISBN 978-1-5723-0088-0.

7. Goleman, Daniel. *The Emotional Brain and Emotional Intelligence: New Insights*. Northampton, Massachusetts, 2011.

8. Wangerin, Jr., Walter. *Mourning into Dancing*. (Grand Rapids, MI: Zondervan Publishing House, 1992), 191.

9. Walton, Charlie. *When There Are No Words: Finding Your Way to Cope with Loss and Grief.* (Ventura, California: Pathfinder Publishing,1999).

10. Charlie Walton died a few years ago but his book is still available at Amazon. I give it away so often that I never have a copy of my own. I highly recommend it.

11. Greenspan, Miriam. *Healing Through the Dark Emotions: The Wisdom of Grief, Fear, and Despair.* (Boston: Shambala Public, Inc., 2003), 96.

12. Chambers, Oswald. *My Utmost for His Highest.* (Grand Rapids, MI:

Discovery House Publishers, 1995). May 22.

13. Lamott, Anne. *Stitches: A Handbook on Meaning, Hope, and Repair.* (Riverhead Books, 2013), 46

14. Kubler-Ross, Elisabeth. *On Death and Dying.* (New York: Scribner,1997).

15. Wangerin, 29.

16. Wangerin, 157.

17. https://www.goodtherapy.org/blog/stages-of-trauma-recovery-what-it-means-to-be-a-survivor-0803155   retrieved 6 June18.

18. Wangerin, 198.

19. https://www.goodtherapy.org/blog/stages-of-trauma-recovery-what-it-means-to-be-a-survivor-0803155

20. Wangerin, 240.

21. Wangerin, 250.

22. Wangerin, 161.

23. https://www.goodtherapy.org/blog/stages-of-trauma-recovery-what-it-means-to-be-a-survivor-0803155

24. Wangerin, 29.

25. Guthrie, Nancy. *The Wisdom of God: Seeing Jesus in the Psalms and Wisdom Books.* (Wheaton, IL: Crossway, 2012), 75-80.

26. Guthrie, 80.

27. Guthrie, 66.

28. Guthrie, 71.

29. Nouwen, Henry. *Turning My Mourning into Dancing.* (Nashville, TN: Thomas Nelson, 2004), 8-9.

30. Chambers, July 6

31. Chambers, July 29.

32. Wolterstorff, Nicholas. *Lament for a Son.* (Grand Rapids, MI: William B. Eerdmans Publishing Co., 1987), 76.

33. Wolterstorff. 71, 72.

34. Wolterstorff. 33.

35. Wolterstorff. 15.

36. Wolterstorff. 22.

37. Wangerin. 160.

38. Lindbergh, Reeve. *No More Words.* (New York: Simon & Schuster, 2001), 15.

39. Chambers, August 10.

40. Two Listeners. *God Calling Journal.* Ed. A.J. Russell. (Uhrichsville, OH: Barbour and Company, Inc., 1953) 218.

41. Loehrer. Michael C. *How to Change a Rotten Attitude: A Manual for Building Virtue and Character in Middle and High School Students.* (Thousand Oaks, California: Corwin Press. Inc., 1998) 166

42. Greenspan, 78.

43. Wangerin, 160

44. Greenspan, 99.

45. Chambers, Oswald. *My Utmost for His Highest.* Jan.2.

46. Karon, Jan. *The Mitford Bedside Companion.* (New York: Penguin Group, 2006). 50.

47. Chambers, Oswald. *My Utmost for His Highest.* Jan. 19

48. Chambers, Oswald. *My Utmost for His Highest.* March 30.

49. Wangerin. 187.

50. Wolterstorff, 67.

51. Chambers, July 28.

52. *Deep Calls to Deep.* "Deep Calls to Deep" www.zoegroup.org

53. Covey, Stephen R. *The Eighth Habit DVD: From Effectiveness to Greatness.* (FranklinCovey Co.: www.the8thhabit.com)

54. *Best of Janet Paschal.* "It Won't Rain Always". Spring House/EMI, 2007

55. Eldredge, John. *Epic.* (Nashville: Thomas Nelson, 2004), 3

56. Eldredge, 5.

57. Kidd, Sue Monk. *When the Heart Waits: Spiritual Direction for Life's Sacred Questions.* (San Francisco: HarperCollins Publishers, 1990). 171

58. Cisneros, Sandra. *Have You Seen Marie?* (New York: Alfred A. Knopf Publishers, 2012). 94

59. Jones, Tony. *The Sacred Way.* (Grand Rapids, MI: Zondervan, 2005)

60. https://www.bcponline.org/DailyOffice/compline.html

61. Eldredge, John. *The Ransomed Heart.* (Nashville: Thomas Nelson, 2005).

62. Dunn, Bill and Leonard, Kathy. *Through a season of grief.* (Nashville: Thomas Nelson, 2004).

63. Tickle, Phyllis. *The Divine Hours: Prayers for Autumn and Wintertime.* (New York: Doubleday, 2000).

64. Eldredge, 31.

65. Eldredge, 33.

66. Eldredge, 53.

67. Lewis, C.S. quoted in *The Ransomed Heart*, 53.

68. Eldredge, 74

69. Eldredge, 75

70. Eldredge, 80.

71. Eldredge, 113.

72. Eldredge, 114.

73. Eldredge, 121.

74. Eldredge, 127.

75. Eldredge, 186.

76. Eldredge, 194.

77. Lewis, C.S. *The Four Loves*. (New York: Harcourt Brace, 1960), 111.

78. Chambers, Feb. 14.

79. Voskamp, Ann. *One Thousand Gifts: A Dare to Live Fully Right Where You Are*. (Grand Rapids: Zondervan, 2010). 11-12.

80. Young, Sarah. *Jesus Calling*. (Nashville: Thomas Nelson, 2004).

81. Voskamp, 12.

82. Voskamp, 93.

83. Voskamp, 112.

84. Voskamp, 113.

85. Voskamp, 114.

86. Voskamp, 121.

87. Voskamp, 59.

88. Young, 80.

89. Lamott, 33.

90. Lamott, 17.

91. Paulus, Trina. *Hope for the Flowers*. (New York: Paulist Press, 1972).

Made in the USA
Lexington, KY
20 December 2018